Open Source Starter Guide
for IBM i Developers

Pete Helgren

MC PRESS

MC Press Online, LLC
Boise, ID 83703 USA

Open Source Starter Guide for IBM i Developers
Pete Helgren

First Edition
First Printing May 2017

MC Press Online, LLC
Corporate Offices: 3695 W. Quail Heights Court, Boise, ID 83703-3861 USA
Sales and Customer Service: (208) 629-7275 ext. 500;
service@mcpressonline.com
Permissions and Bulk/Special Orders: mcbooks@mcpressonline.com

www.mcpressonline.com • www.mc-store.com

ISBN: 978-1-58347-495-2

Acknowledgments

It is an African proverb that says "It takes a village to raise a child." Although I had nowhere near a "village" helping me, a "child" in programming, I have always felt the presence of the IBM i/Midrange community for whom this book is written. What a "village" it is! It is awesome to be a part of something like that community, and I thank them for their encouragement. I also want to thank Tony Cairns and IBM, Aaron Bartell, and Andrea Ribuoli for responding to my inane questions. I know them all well, and it is always a pleasure to work with them.

On a personal note, I am very thankful for my long-suffering wife who over the years has put up with "hang on, I almost have it working" delays. Every person should be blessed with such patient love. Thanks, Debbie.

None of this is remotely possible without a God who animates and directs me. We are made in His image, and I love it when His creativity breaks through my ignorance. "With man this is impossible, but with God all things are possible" (Matt. 19:26). Yeah, it's like that. Thanks be to God!

Contents

Preface

I have worked for Bible Study Fellowship (BSF) for four years as of this writing, and I look forward to coming to work every day! And it is not just because I get to work with people I love, for a God I love, but also because I get to do a job I love.

I *love* to write code, break code, learn new things about code, talk about code, debate about code, everything! Every day I get to try something I have never tried before, and I have a computing system that makes it possible: IBM i on Power. It's about as close to "processing heaven" as you can get, IMHO. I do understand that not everybody sees it that way. There are folks who see their work as "just a job" and can't wait to get home, or for the lucky ones, push back from the desk at a home office, and they are done. It's a job, nothing more. There may have been a time when coding was new and exciting, but now, after writing RPG for 20 years, the spark is gone. It's just a job.

I think part of the reason we can fall into the "it's just a job" trap is because we *have* been doing the same thing for so long, and perhaps we don't, or aren't allowed to, learn anything. And the Internet facilitates, in some ways, our *lack* of learning (yeah, you read that right!).

Not long after I started working at BSF, I was sorting through the morning tech support email and came across this:

> *Who ever devised these questions did not use a straight forward approach. We are studying Matthew, who cares what Mark says or the old testament says.... I just look up the verses to get the answers not to learn anything. It is a means to an end.*

Wow! I was stunned for a minute, not only because the tone was kind of negative (not totally unusual, but we *are* a Christian organization), but because I had this epiphany about learning and the Internet: we don't learn anything; we just use it to get the answers! When I took stock of my own behavior, yes, I used the Internet as an "answer machine," and I really wasn't learning anything. Time to change.

So I used the usual tools I have to guide me: "Debugging is the beginning of wisdom" and "It isn't science; it's technology." Debugging is not just getting and finding a bug, but learning something in the process, usually how the technology *really* works. And I see writing code as more art than science. You start with a blank screen, and by typing stuff, you can create beautiful pictures, fun games, useful tools. What other job gives you that level of creativity? I believe that we are created to flourish and grow as humans, and learning—lifelong learning—is the key.

When I was asked to write this book, I said yes, even though I had never written a book before (which may become painfully evident). On the face of it, it is a dumb idea in the 21st century to write something that will probably be out of date before it is published. So I decided to put some fun into the effort and also to really walk through the details, pointing out where I was confused after my first "get an answer" effort yielded a solution that I didn't understand. And man, I want you to have some fun! Life is way too short to live only in the confines of a box of our own creating, limiting ourselves because we are doing what we always do. I hope I can add a little "flourish" to your life. This book focuses on the "open source garden of goodness" that is available to developers who are creative and courageous enough to step outside the box, to look for more than just answers, and to learn for the joy of it. I hope your journey is enjoyable.

I am a Christian, and I work for a Christian organization, so I have started each chapter with a bit of "ancient wisdom" to start you thinking in each chapter. May you get as much joy in learning as I did in writing!

"Gray hair is a crown of splendor; it is attained in the way of righteousness" (Prov. 16:31—*love* it!).

1

IBM i and Open Source

If you are new to IBM i, then welcome! I would guess though, that if you picked up this book, you probably already have an IBM i, or access to one, and you are hoping to leverage some of that IBM i goodness because …

1. You want to have fun trying something new.
2. You have a project and want to try something different (from a little different to *way* different).
3. You've been given a mandate to learn something new.
4. You're curious what all the "buzz" is about.
5. All of the above.

If you are new to open source software, frequently referred to as OSS, then welcome again! In addition to the previous list, I would guess you might also have the following in mind:

1. You want to add to your repertoire of skills with something more "cutting edge."
2. You want to add to those skills with a low cost of entry.
3. You have a specific project in mind, and an open source solution has been proposed.

Why Open Source on IBM i?

You have come to the right place because, from my slightly skewed perspective, the IBM i is a perfectly designed open source machine. Why do I think that? Here's why:

- It's running the POWER8 chip. Best silicon in the universe!
- It has all the "legacy" (I really hate that word, but it fits) languages that solid business logic can be written in: RPG, COBOL, C, C++ (even FORTRAN).
- The ILE and PASE environments are two environments that can share resources seamlessly, which means AIX binaries can be leveraged with RPG business logic.
- Can you find a better database than DB2 on IBM i? I doubt it! And on IBM i, it's completely integrated into the OS. No database admin needed.
- Stable, secure OS. No patch Tuesdays. No classic buffer overflow exploits. You can sleep at night (or at your desk during the day, like I do).
- There is a whole list of IBM-provided and supported OSS that will run on IBM i "out of the box."

Ask any IBM i programmers or any IT managers running IBM i in their shop, and they can easily add to the list above. Then, on top of it all, you have a close-knit, vibrant community that not only includes IBM i owners but IBMers themselves. How many Microsoft executives have you spent time with at a user conference? Can you name Microsoft's current Windows Chief Architect? How often do you get a nearly immediate email back from a Microsoft developer? How many Microsoft developers do you know who lurk on popular mailing lists and pop in with answers? I really don't have anything against Microsoft. But the IBM i ecosystem is just awesome! Community members and IBMers all love the same platform for the same reason. It just doesn't get any better than that! Yeah, I'm spoiled and I know it, but I'm still amazed by how engaged IBM as a company is with the community.

It's All About the Community

Flash back to 1995. I'm sitting in a big tent in Redmond, waiting for the Windows 95 Launch to start. As a Windows 95 beta tester, I have been fully involved with every step of testing the operating system, loving the community effort. I even wore a vest made of beta installation CDs. Folks took my picture. That was my "15 minutes of fame!"

Microsoft has *long* promised to get me the collateral that backs up my presence at the launch ... but alas! They are too big to follow through (apparently).

At the time, I loved Microsoft for all the reasons I love IBM i and the community today: engagement and connection with a community with purpose. Very cool. Well, Microsoft got bigger and more distant and impersonal for me while the IBM i community got better and more "communal." IBM hasn't yet lost its mojo when it comes to the IBM i platform and the community. And for anything to retain a personal feel in this electronic, Internet-connected world is an amazing feat. The IBM i community hasn't succumbed to the siren of "all virtual" yet. You can still rub shoulders with everyone from IBM executives to propeller heads at conferences across the world. If you get the chance, *do it!*

I know what you're thinking ... something like this: "Yeah, it's cool, but *any* operating system can run open source stuff, and there are still plenty of in-person events I can go to. What's the big deal about IBM i?" Well, OK, you *can* run PHP, Ruby/Rails, Python, Node.js, and plenty of other stuff on LUW (Linux UNIX Windows). I do it all the time while I am developing applications. But I would claim that you can't do it with as much security and scalability and with the performance the POWER chip brings to the table. Having survived the Great Recession, I am as happy to have a job as anyone, and I am a big fan of full employment, but I don't see either the efficiency or economy of running a server farm. Granted, with clustering, load balancing, failover, and other mitigation techniques, running a farm of Linux or Windows servers can keep your uptime *up*! But who wants the aggravation? Not me! So IBM i has been a great timesaver. I bounce my IBM i maybe twice a year, usually because there is some essential add-on I need, and in order to get what I want, I have to apply a Technology Refresh, basically a version step upgrade, and then bounce. But I can't tell you the last time a "critical security update" was issued for my IBM i. It's just that good.

OK. You probably already have an IBM i. Weren't those paragraphs above stoking your fire about what a great platform we have? Get out there and tell folks. Not just because you are an IBM i "bigot" (we may be opinionated but not bigoted) but because you want people to have *fun* in their IT work! You aren't?! Then read the rest of this book. There is a boatload of goodness that is waiting for you in the IBM i open source garden. Jump in!

2

The PASE Environment

PASE (pronounced *paze*) has been around since IBM i and its predecessors have been running 64-bit architecture. Even before PowerPC! Officially, PASE is an acronym for Portable Application Solutions Environment (after being initially called the Private Address Space Environment). In my book, it's the Pretty Awesome Software Environment, where it seems like just about anything is possible.

PASE is important because it's like Oz in *The Wizard of Oz*, where you suddenly leave the black and white world of RPG and then land, sometimes with a thud, into the color-filled world of open source. It is a beautiful garden of possibilities, and I am *very* thankful the folks at IBM made the brilliant decision to include it as part of OS/400, i5/OS, and now, IBM i.

But what the heck *is* it? It's an integrated runtime environment that allows you to run most AIX programs unaltered, right there on IBM i! It isn't an emulation environment, nor is it interpreted. It is simply an AIX runtime with access to the full range of IBM i resources. It's designed for accommodation, particularly for C and C++ programs, but also a full range of others. And it's very cool! So I'll take you on a journey through this amazing "software garden," and hopefully I'll plant a few seeds along the way.

PASE and ILE

There are really worlds that live in complete harmony on IBM i (for example, the ILE world and the PASE world). And the remarkable thing is that, rather than taking the dueling-brothers approach (you know, Cain and Abel, Jacob and Esau ...), these worlds peacefully coexist, sharing many resources across what would seem to be an impenetrable wall. To get started, here is just *some* of what is shared in these environments:

- User/group profiles
- Process structures
- Thread structures
- Database (DB2)
- Integrated File System (IFS)
- System Licensed Internal Code (SLIC) kernel, below Machine Interface (MI)
- PowerPC machine instruction set (no emulation)
- Most everything ... even "underwear"—such as hardware resources (disk, memory, CPU, and so on)

The IBM i really does have quite a unique architecture, and you are welcome to grub around on the Internet for more information. However, I think the success of the architecture and the reason that PASE and ILE live so comfortably together is that the operating system lives well above the hardware; so much of what goes on with processor changes has little to no effect on the existing running applications. Sure, they run *faster*, but they also still run.

When was the last time you ran a DOS program from 1985 in Windows 10? OK, who would *want* to? Sometimes I hear complaints that folks make the latest POWER8 system look like a dinosaur because they are still running apps written in 1990 (or earlier) on IBM i. "Pshaw," I say! Move some applications that run in PHP, or Ruby/Rails out of the constantly patched environments of Windows and get settled in on PASE or ILE on IBM i. Free up some admin time to have some fun, for goodness sakes. Life is too short to spend it patching security holes …, but let's not go there right now. Classic buffer overflow exploits that fall over into some privilege-escalation bug just don't happen in the PASE Garden of Eden. You are safe and secure there.

The beauty of sharing in PASE and ILE makes it the perfect place to leverage rock-solid business apps with nice, cutting-edge Web technologies like Node.js. What are the differences between the two? Let's look at Table 2.1 below.

Table 2.1: Differences Between the PASE and ILE Environments	
PASE	**ILE**
/QOpenSys/IBM	LIB/FILE.MBR
Debuggers "unlimited"	Debuggers "very limited"
Allows code generation	No code generation
Uses syscalls to kernel	Uses MI to kernel
ASCII	EBCDIC
Float, double, int, char	Adds packed, zoned
Main program (/PATH/mypgm)	ILE *PGM
Shared objects (lib.a, lib.so)	ILE *SRVPGM
Use env vars (PATH, LIBPATH)	Use *LIBL
Shells (qp2term, ssh, bash…)	QSH (*PGMs)
Call ILE (_PGMCALL, _ILECALL)	Call PASE (Qp2RunPase, Qp2CallPase, QP2SHELL)

Even with these differences, there is much similarity. What I find in common particularly *within* each environment is the way you can leverage programs to work together. ILE allows for multiple languages and program objects to play well together. The same applies to PASE. Combined, PASE and ILE take advantage of the power of IBM i and maximize the flexibility in which you can approach building solutions. And, as much as I love to play within that garden of flexibility, the real value is that when it comes to running a business, you have a broad world of programming and solutions at your fingertips.

Figure 2.1 illustrates what I have been talking about so far.

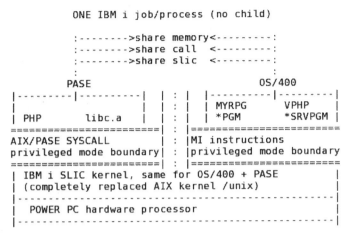

Figure 2.1: PASE and ILE commonalities and differences

Installing PASE

No biggie here. You install using the Install Licensed Programs menu or command (you choose). The product is 5770-SS1 Option 33. It is a free licensed program. (In my humble opinion, this thing should come installed with the base OS; it seems to be an increasingly essential component of *everything* I run into.) Keep it current with PTFs. Actually, as a runtime, I really never gave it a second thought after I installed it. Like the IBM i OS, it just runs.

PASE Applications

Remember that 5733OPS ships with a bunch of PASE-ready applications. They are already compiled for PASE, most likely for AIX version 5.1, which is the lowest common denominator for all currently supported versions of IBM i. Table 2.2 shows the "matrix of support" when it comes to AIX and IBM i.

Table 2.2: AIX Version Support on IBM i					
AIX Release (32 or 64 bit)	IBM i V5R3	IBM i V5R4	IBM i 6.1	IBM i 7.1	IBM i 7.2
5.1	X	X	X	X	X
5.2		X	X	X	X
5.3		X	X	X	X
6.1				X	X
7.1					X

Theoretically (remember this is technology, not science), you can take binaries compiled for the corresponding AIX release and drop them into PASE, and they *might* work. Several websites have binaries ready for download and installation. The Young i Professionals website (*yips.idevcloud.com/wiki*) is one, and the *perzl.org* website is another. Again, for what this book addresses, there really isn't a need to go anywhere else; you'll get the binaries when you install 5733OPS and corresponding PTFs. But if you have a favorite AIX program or package you want to use, give it a try. You never know until you try.

You can also compile your own binaries if you have an adventurous spirit and a lack of good common sense. I can't remember exactly what year it was, maybe 2004 or so, that I was compiling PHP in PASE during the Thanksgiving holiday. It was an excruciating learning curve for a "seat of the pants" RPG programmer like me, but the gleeful happy dance that resulted from a clean compile was worth the effort. Nothing like trying something new and finally getting it to work! I just *love* this stuff. So, if a hack like me could figure it out from scratch over a decade ago, you certainly can do it today. There is plenty of help from many very good minds that know the PASE environment and can steer you through the ins and outs of compiling C code (it's mostly C with some C++). The GNU compiler is now included as part of the 5733OPS license code offering. It's practically *begging* you to try!

PASE apps can be written in C, C++, Fortran, or PowerPC assembler (!). PASE apps use the same binary executable format as AIX PowerPC applications, which is cool and very compatible. Those PASE binaries run in an IBM i job, and as I mentioned, PASE programs use IBM i system functions, such as file systems, security, and sockets. So, again, this is not an operating system within an operating system. The AIX runtime isn't emulated; it is running on top of SLIC, just like RPG or COBOL, so not only do you have the full range of AIX APIs available, but they run fast. The best of both worlds. There is a broad subset of AIX technology available in PASE, including:

- Standard C and C++ runtime (both threadsafe and non-threadsafe)
- Fortran runtime (both threadsafe and non-threadsafe)
- pthreads threading package
- iconv services for data conversion (handy and available in ILE)
- Berkeley Software Distributions (BSD) equivalent support
- X Window System client support with Motif widget set

- Pseudo terminal (PTY) support

You have your choice of shells, so you can be opinionated about such things (I'm a BASH guy myself). And if you happen to spend a bit of time in Linux distros, like I do, it eventually becomes as comfortable as that overstuffed chair you lounge in. You can enter the PASE world from the IBM i command line by calling QP2TERM, but why would you want to run a terminal emulator from within a terminal emulator? And the shell is terrible (OK, see, now I am opinionated about shells). Typically, you'd have a happier experience using SSH to access the PASE environment, and I highly recommend you do so. The open source Secure Shell (SSH) and Telnet client PuTTY is what I use, but there are several, and any of them will do the job.

Using PASE

You can call PASE programs from the ILE world, and vice versa. Table 2.3 shows a list of the commands that take you from one world to another (although the jump really isn't that far).

Table 2.3: PASE to ILE and Vice Versa	
PASE to ILE	**ILE to PASE**
_PGMCALL—Call *PGM	Qp2RunPase—Run PASE program (main)
_ILELOADX—Load *SRVPGM	Qp2dlopen—Load PASE module (*.a, *.so)
_ILESYMX—Find export symbol (proc)	Qp2dlsym—Find export symbol (function)
_ILECALLX—Call export procedure	Qp2CallPase—Call PASE function
_CVTSSP—Convert space pointer	Qp2dlclose—Close load
_CVTTS64—Convert teraspace addr	Qp2dlerror—Get last error dl operation
_GETTS64—Get teraspace addr	Qp2malloc—Alloc PASE heap memory
GETTS64SPP—Get teraspace addr	Qp2free—Free PASE heap memory
_GETTS64M—Get multiple teraspace	Qp2SignalPase—Post signal to PASE
_SETSPP—Set space pointer	Qp2EndPase—End PASE
SETSPPTS64—Set space pointer	Qp2jobCCSID—Get PASE job CCSID (last)
_SETSPPM—Set multiple space pointers	Qp2paseCCSID—Get PASE CCSID (last)
systemCL()—Run CL command	Qp2ptrsize—Get ptr size running PASE job

It's actually pretty simple. Take a look at this CL program that runs the ls program in PASE (ls is the "list files" command similar to dir). It's the "cheater's" way to do it because I am just invoking the PASE shell and running the command within it.

```
PGM
DCL VAR(&CMD) TYPE(*CHAR) LEN(20) VALUE('/QOpenSys/bin/ls')
DCL VAR(&PARM1) TYPE(*CHAR) LEN(10) VALUE('/')
DCL VAR(&NULL) TYPE(*CHAR) LEN(1) VALUE(X'00')
CHGVAR VAR(&CMD) VALUE(&CMD *TCAT &NULL)
CHGVAR VAR(&PARM1) VALUE(&PARM1 *TCAT &NULL)
CALL PGM(QP2SHELL) PARM(&CMD &PARM1)
ENDIT:
ENDPGM
```

The flip side is to invoke an ILE CL program from PASE. That takes a C language program, compiled in PASE:

```
/* sampleCL.c
example to demonstrate use of sampleCL to run a CL command
Compile with a command similar to the following.
xlc -o sampleCL -I /whatever/pase -bI:/whatever/pase/as400_libc.exp
sampleCL.c
Example program using QP2SHELL() follows.
call qp2shell ('sampleCL' 'wrkactjob') */
#include <stdio.h>
#include <stdlib.h>
#include <errno.h>
#include <as400_types.h> /* PASE header */
#include <as400_protos.h> /* PASE header */
void main(int argc, char* argv[])
{
int rc;
if (argc!=2)
{
printf("usage: %s \"CL command\"\n", argv[0]);
exit(1);
}
```

Continued

```
printf("running CL command: \"%s\"\n", argv[1]);
/* process the CL command */
rc = systemCL(argv[1], /* use first parameter for CL command */
SYSTEMCL_MSG_STDOUT
SYSTEMCL_MSG_STDERR ); /* collect messages */
printf("systemCL returned %d. \n", rc);
if (rc != 0)
{
perror("systemCL");
exit(rc);
}
}
```

You may not be a C programmer, but I bet you can follow the coding here. You have a standard set of C header files—such as stdio.h, stdlib.h, and errno.h—and then some PASE-specific headers that reference the APIs and constants needed to make the CL call. In this case, you aren't "shelling into" the IBM i command line and back out. The results will be piped directly back to the C program and displayed on the command line.

These examples, and a host of others, can be found in the IBM Knowledge Center PDF, *IBM PASE for i* (*https://www.ibm.com/support/knowledgecenter/ssw_ibm_i_71/rzalf/ rzalfmstpdf.htm*). It's pretty readable and has enough examples to get you started. My preference is for agonizing detail, explaining stuff that even the author thinks the audience should know, but this document is a little light on details in some places. If you can get the examples to compile, though, that learning curve alone should be a good grounding.

The great thing about PASE is that after a while, you forget that you are in foreign territory. Quite a few of us grew up in a command-line world, whether it was IBM i or DOS. It is now the cool place to be (a GUI is so 1990s!). My 29-year-old son talks about how cool the "PowerShell" is in Windows. "It's amazing what you can do with scripting!" he says. I say, "Son, I used to write batch files and CL commands in my sleep!" What was old is new again. The command line is dead! Long live the command line!

PASE is where all the action is in the IBM i open source software world. It's a lush garden of goodness! Enjoy!

3

The Integrated Language Environment (ILE)

The audience for this book is RPG programmers, so what are you doing reading this chapter? Move on! You know this stuff! For those who don't, however, I am going to briefly review some of the basic concepts of ILE. Why? Because you'll get a glimpse, just a small glimpse, of the power that has been beautifully designed into the IBM i operating system.

We have an environment supporting multiple languages, yet, rather than falling into a Tower of Babel rabble, ILE gets everyone talking to one another without any acrimony. This is *very* cool stuff, and most of the key components have been around for decades. If you want an exhaustive, deep dive into ILE programming, or you just need help falling asleep, pick up the *ILE Concepts* Redbook (SC41-5606-10).

ILE's Origins

ILE, the environment we have known and loved for years, grew out of a need for a more heterogeneous environment for programming on what was then the AS/400. The whole goal was to improve upon the Original Program Model (OPM), where dynamic program calls were made from one program to another. Each OPM program could be "modular" in the sense that it could perform a specific purpose, but the whole concept of binding dependent programs together into a module or another program was just a pipe dream. Building completely modular code with each module performing a single procedure or a series of procedures just wasn't possible.

Much of the code I worked with early on (late '80s to early '90s) was a "framework," but it was a framework of compile-time /copy directives that a pre-processor would build in a temporary source file, compile, and then deploy. It was slick at the time, but debugging was a bear (hang on to those temp source files!). If you wrote RPG, then the stack was RPG (and maybe CL). If you wrote COBOL, then your stack was COBOL. It was, to say the least, a bit constraining. OPM led to Extended Program Model (EPM), which ended up being an interim solution as ILE was implemented soon after.

I can't say exactly what the rationale was for heading in the heterogeneous direction when so many platforms at the time were single language, single operating system, but my guess is that the continuing popularity of languages like COBOL, BASIC, C, and C++ alongside RPG and CL was the impetus for supporting compilers and runtimes that supported them. Maybe people were saying something like this: "Dude! I want to run my COBOL on a rippin' fast machine like an AS/400!" I have no idea! I was an RPG programmer with a dangerous bit of Fortran and BASIC programming in the bag, and frankly, just learning RPG was enough. But the predecessors of the AS/400 had multilingual capabilities, and I guess that the propeller heads in Toronto and the hardware folks in Rochester just kept thinking up ways to leverage all the capabilities on the AS/400, just like the open source efforts going on with IBM i today. Innovation has never been an issue with the IBM i family. But the multiple languages and the capability led naturally, I think, to figuring out how to make it all work together.

Modularity and Binding

The initial steps focused on allowing code to be more modular. So the module concept came along, and those modules, while not runnable themselves, could be bound into service programs or bound into programs that *were* runnable. This ILE concept *should* be part of an RPG programmer's DNA, and my guess is that for large programs with many moving parts, you are building your programs in a modular way.

Why would anyone want to break programs into service programs with procedures and subprocedures when you could just knock out a single OPM program and be done with it? The key is code reuse! In Ruby/Rails there is a concept called DRY, which stands for "Don't Repeat Yourself." In the early days of ILE, RPG was just beginning to DRY out versus the old WET ("Write, Experiment, and Tweak") method that I used until I got something to work ... the second time! We think in modular terms today, but it took the implementation of ILE plus the ability to think differently to change programming, even programming RPG, for the better.

Since you have all these disparate parts in programs, service programs, and modules, there's probably a bell ringing at the back of your head reminding you of something— like, how do I keep track of all this? How do I know which pieces, parts, and *fused parts* fit together? Yikes! Well, there's a binding language for that, and it defines how to pull all the disparate pieces into a functioning whole. It is yet another component called a *binding directory*, which lists which parts go where. If you have a service program that has 20 procedures but your program needs only one of them, that one procedure can be bound into your program, making it more compact and efficient at run time. Yeah, each component I have listed so far creates a bit more work and one more thing to attend to, but the return is great. You just have to keep track of what procedures you have in what service programs or modules, and basically you can have a Chinese buffet of programming, picking and choosing, and then binding it into a whole.

The Benefits of ILE's Integration

ILE is a tool that can help you organize your code, make you think more carefully about actual program functionality, and give you some reusable components. Not bad, but you could have been simulating that as best you could, even in an OPM program. But what if your shop isn't *just* an RPG shop? What if you have COBOL and C and C++ programmers, and they have all embraced ILE concepts and write ILE code on your IBM i? Or even if you don't have other non-RPG ILE programmers, maybe you know other programmers in other languages in other shops, and they're willing to share their stuff with you. There is a small but growing community of ILE programmers who *do* share their code. What if you tripped across a very nice bit of code in ILE C that you wanted to use? What then? Use it! Because ILE is ILE is ILE, so you can bind and call C from COBOL or RPG and vice versa.

That is where ILE really shines! It's a better, more efficient way of programming, and even if you're in a single-language track, you will benefit by getting on the ILE bandwagon. Remember that lowercase "i" in IBM i? Remember what it stands for? Integration! And what does the uppercase "I" in ILE stand for? Integrated! How many more times do you need to hear that wonderful word in any form? It opens up a whole new world.

I'm going to revisit the idea that the *only* reason for grabbing someone else's code is to save you some time or money on a project. Not so. You also learn quite a bit about your own programming skills—and perhaps a better way to code—by looking at someone's COBOL or C code. And that is the best part about writing code and sharing code: you learn more! I highly recommend you wade through some code in an ILE language where RPG makes a call to C functions. Better yet, do it in free-format RPG. As languages evolve and take on attributes of other languages, you would do well to spend some time kicking the tires of another ILE language.

This discussion is just to whet your appetite for more "i": integration! That's what the open source world is all about. This chapter hardly scratches the surface. We didn't even touch upon activation groups, teraspaces, debugging, shared memory storage, and so much more. But you are an RPG programmer and probably have a list of things you'd like to teach *me*.

4

The Beast That Is XMLSERVICE

Perhaps not quite like the Watcher in the Water in *The Lord of the Rings* but equally mysterious is XMLSERVICE: the program framework that provides "glue" between the PASE world and the OSS world. XMLSERVICE has been around since the early days of PHP on i to make PHP truly useful on IBM i. I say to make it useful because although there are plenty of off-the-shelf PHP applications that you can install on IBM i and immediately make use of (e.g., Joomla, WordPress, osCommerce, Drupal), none of them take advantage of the main reason you'd want to run open source on IBM i: your business logic and database. You're leveraging the security of IBM i as well, but let's face it: you can always run that stuff on something like Ubuntu, Red Hat, or Suse, and it will rock on the Power platform. You want access to the investment you made in writing RPG logic using the DB2 for i database. XMLSERVICE will get you there because it is written specifically to access to resources in the "native" space of IBM i. But it isn't all that easy to wrap your head around. You'll be communicating with that native side using XML as your lingua franca, and frankly, XML isn't all that easy to deal with. The really good news is that JSON will be supported soon (October 2016?), so it may be *much* easier at that point to see and understand the interchange between the two worlds because JSON is easier to "read," in my humble opinion.

Installation

If you do an Internet search on "XMLSERVICE", you'll probably end up at the YiPs website (*yips.idevcloud.com*) because that is where XMLSERVICE began its open source life. Although bits and pieces of it are now beginning to migrate to other websites, YiPs is still a good starting place. Installation is pretty straightforward and trouble-free; I had it downloaded and installed in less than 15 minutes. The straight-up installation is easy. Of all OSS products, this one is pretty simple. You can download the zip file, which contains the XMLSERVICE library and source, from either the YiPs or Bitbucket websites. Download the file, and unzip the contents. Create a save file called XMLSERVICE on your IBM i in QGPL, and then FTP the file from your PC to the IBM i. Use RSTLIB (Restore Library) to restore the XMLSERVICE library. Once you add XMLSERVICE to your library list, you can run:

```
CRTCLPGM PGM(XMLSERVICE/CRTXML) SRCFILE(XMLSERVICE/QCLSRC)
call crtxml -- XMLSERVICE library only
```

And then run:

```
CRTCLPGM PGM(XMLSERVICE/CRTTEST) SRCFILE(XMLSERVICE/QCLSRC)
call crttest
```

And if you are on an IBM i release of V6R0 or greater, run:

```
CRTCLPGM PGM(XMLSERVICE/CRTTEST6) SRCFILE(XMLSERVICE/QCLSRC)
call crttest6
```

This will create the test programs you can call to get familiar with XMLSERVICE. For REST, you'll need to make sure that the HTTP users can access the programs, so you run the following commands to grant object authority to the library and programs:

```
CHGAUT OBJ('/qsys.lib/XMLSERVICE.lib') USER(QTMHHTTP) DTAAUT(*RWX)
OBJAUT(*ALL) SUBTREE(*ALL)
CHGAUT OBJ('/qsys.lib/XMLSERVICE.lib') USER(QTMHHTP1) DTAAUT(*RWX)
OBJAUT(*ALL) SUBTREE(*ALL)
```

The installation instructions also list some "Alternative compiles." Basically, there are other providers of XMLSERVICE that have the library included with their deliverables. So PHP, with its multiple versions from Zend, PowerRuby, and even IBM directly through PTF can supply the library. In my opinion, the best place to go for the latest and greatest would be either the YiPs site or the Bitbucket site.

Note: I can pretty much guarantee you that the installation instructions will change over time, and probably the location of the open source projects will change as well. Check for the latest changes on either the *common.org* website or my website (*www.petesworkshop. com*).

The installation instructions then go on to give you Apache directives for using XMLSERVICE with a RESTful interface. The Apache directives for a "vanilla" install look like this:

```
ScriptAlias /cgi-bin/ /QSYS.LIB/XMLSERVICE.LIB/
<Directory /QSYS.LIB/XMLSERVICE.LIB/>
  AllowOverride None
  order allow,deny
  allow from all
  SetHandler cgi-script
  Options +ExecCGI
</Directory>
```

If you are not familiar with Apache directives, this can look a little cryptic. CGI is an acronym for the Common Gateway Interface, which was designed as a standard very early on in the World Wide Web (WWW) life cycle (1993) and provided a standardized way that a command could be processed through an HTTP server. Basically the directive above examines a URL passed to the server that contains /cgi-bin/ and will map that program call to the XMLSERVICE library for processing. The RPG-based CGIDEV2 library uses the same mechanism to process HTML in an RPG program.

Next Steps

Figuring out what to do next is a bigger challenge. But let's start with some of the conceptual stuff that we'll need to make a reasonable go at successfully *using* what we just installed.

You'll probably see the diagram in Figure 4.1 if you go to the YiPs site and navigate to the XMLSERVICE page.

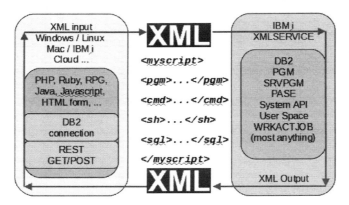

Figure 4.1: XMLSERVICE data interchange layer

This is a nice little graphic, but what exactly is it trying to tell you? Basically it illustrates that the open source world (all the stuff on the left) can communicate with and execute code and commands in the IBM i world (all the stuff on the right) and use XML to pass the data to and from those worlds. Also, encapsulated in the little blue "pill"-shaped boxes (*obviously* created by a guy over 50) are the methods that can be used to communicate to the IBM i.

It makes good sense when you think about it: the two most "open" methods for accessing system resources are through Web servers and database servers. Actually, those are also two vectors for security exploits, so we are just leveraging the "information pipelines" that most servers have. I am *not* saying that XMLSERVICE is inherently insecure; it isn't when used wisely. What I *am* saying is that if you were going to build a connection into system resources, why not use connection methods that already exist? So the REST interface uses the HTTP server, and the other method will use the DB2 for i server. Sweet!

Tony Cairns of IBM posted this to the Bitbucket project issues (re JSON). It is instructive, I think, about what is going on in XMLSERVICE:

"Essentially XMLSERVICE is a compiler, where in the 'user' feeds XML (or JSON), which is just a big string, that needs to be 'marshalled' into real nested data structures with real values and real pointers, then, load/activates a PGM/SRVPGM (other), and calls [it], followed by a reverse of process back into string again (out pops XML/JSON)."

If you know Tony, he is incredibly terse in his posts, but the basic unpacking of his posts reflects what's in the diagram: the XML with the call parameters and data is passed to XMLSERVICE that marshals it to the environment in which it will be executed.

In order to communicate, XMLSERVICE expects a particular format for the data being sent to the IBM i and will return the response in a particular format as well.

The following code includes a subset of data types supported in XMLSERVICE, but they are probably the most familiar to RPG programmers. You can see how a data type is represented in the XML element:

```
C types           RPG types          XMLSERVICE types           SQL types

packed        D mydec     12p 2   <data type='12p2'/>        DECIMAL(12,2)
zoned         D myzone    12s 2   <data type='12s2'/>        NUMERIC(12,2)
float         D myfloat    4f     <data type='4f2'/>         FLOAT
real/double   D myreal     8f     <data type='8f4'/>         REAL
binary        D mybin    (any)    <data type='9b'>F1F2F3</data>
                                                             BINARY
hole (no out) D myhole   (any)    <data type='40h'/>
boolean       D mybool     1n     <data type='4a'/>          CHAR(4)
time          D mytime     T      <data type='8A'>09.45.29</data>
                                                             TIME timfmt(*iso)
timestamp     D mystamp    Z      <data type='26A'>2011-12-29-12.45.29
                                    .000000</data>           TIMESTAMP
date          D mydate     D      <data type='10A'>2009-05-11</data>
                                                             DATE datfmt(*iso)
```

A typical call to a program or a command on IBM i is pretty simple, and I have sorted out the stuff that tends to repeat for each call from the stuff that changes most every time. Let's start with something simple. (By the way, these examples are from the YiPs site and, frankly, can be a bit challenging.)

XMLSERVICE Examples

We are going to stick with the easiest examples to start. There are some very good examples all around the Web, but let me show you what I did to start.

First Step: Prepare the Apache Server

Going back to the installation steps in the previous section, there is an example of the Apache directive you need to have in order for the CGI interface to find and execute the XMLSERVICE programs. Using the HTTP Administrator Web page on your IBM i—which is typically living at *http://YourIBMiIP:2001*, create a new Apache server instance: from the **All Servers** tab, choose **Create HTTP Server**. Give it a name and description, then click **Next**. Use the default *Server root*, or point it to somewhere in your IFS you want the files to reside, and click **Next**. Use the default document root, or again, point it somewhere you want it to reside, and click **Next**.

On the IP and port selections, you may want to give it some careful thought. You can only have a single port listening on an IP address on your IBM i. By default, you are given the option to listen on all IPs, which is fine as long as you don't have any conflicting ports on *all* your IPs. By default, HTTP traffic is directed to port 80, but for internal testing you can use any non-allocated port you want. Typically, it will be a port above 1024 and maybe much higher, depending upon the TCP/IP services your IBM i supports. Ports go all the way up to 65535, and the range from 49152–65535 is specifically designated as private/ephemeral ports. If you run the command NETSTAT *CNN and use F14 to see the list of actively used ports on your IBM i, you can choose something that is non-conflicting. I chose 7070 in my case because it is easy to remember and unused on my box.

You can click **Next** and make choices about logging, but eventually you'll see the **Finish** button, and you can be done with it. A "pristine" newly created file will look like this:

```
# Configuration originally created by Create HTTP Server wizard on Wed
Aug 17 18:43:54 CDT 2016
Listen *:7070
DocumentRoot /www/xmlserver/htdocs
TraceEnable Off
Options -FollowSymLinks
LogFormat "%h %T %l %u %t \"%r\" %>s %b \"%{Referer}i\" \"%{User-Agent}
i\"" combined
LogFormat "%{Cookie}n \"%r\" %t" cookie
LogFormat "%{User-agent}i" agent
LogFormat "%{Referer}i -> %U" referer
LogFormat "%h %l %u %t \"%r\" %>s %b" common
LogMaint logs/error_log 7 0
SetEnvIf "User-Agent" "Mozilla/2" nokeepalive
SetEnvIf "User-Agent" "JDK/1\.0" force-response-1.0
SetEnvIf "User-Agent" "Java/1\.0" force-response-1.0
SetEnvIf "User-Agent" "RealPlayer 4\.0" force-response-1.0
SetEnvIf "User-Agent" "MSIE 4\.0b2;" nokeepalive
SetEnvIf "User-Agent" "MSIE 4\.0b2;" force-response-1.0
<Directory />
    Require all denied
</Directory>
<Directory /www/xmlserver/htdocs>
    Require all granted
</Directory>
```

You really don't have to understand all that in order to use the configuration, but you will have to modify it. Remember those essential directives we needed, which I mentioned in the installation step? Well, it's time to use them. After you've modified the file, it should look like this:

```
# Configuration originally created by Create HTTP Server wizard on Wed
Aug 10 18:25:22 CDT 2016
                                                          Continued
```

```
Listen *:7070
DocumentRoot /www/xmlserver/htdocs
TraceEnable Off
Options -FollowSymLinks
LogFormat "%h %T %l %u %t \"%r\" %>s %b \"%{Referer}i\" \"%{User-Agent}
i\"" combined
LogFormat "%{Cookie}n \"%r\" %t" cookie
LogFormat "%{User-agent}i" agent
LogFormat "%{Referer}i -> %U" referer
LogFormat "%h %l %u %t \"%r\" %>s %b" common
CustomLog logs/access_log combined
LogMaint logs/access_log 7 0
LogMaint logs/error_log 7 0
SetEnvIf "User-Agent" "Mozilla/2" nokeepalive
SetEnvIf "User-Agent" "JDK/1\.0" force-response-1.0
SetEnvIf "User-Agent" "Java/1\.0" force-response-1.0
SetEnvIf "User-Agent" "RealPlayer 4\.0" force-response-1.0
SetEnvIf "User-Agent" "MSIE 4\.0b2;" nokeepalive
SetEnvIf "User-Agent" "MSIE 4\.0b2;" force-response-1.0
ScriptAlias /cgi-bin/ /QSYS.LIB/XMLSERVICE.LIB/
<Directory /QSYS.LIB/XMLSERVICE.LIB/>
  AllowOverride None
  order allow,deny
  allow from all
  SetHandler cgi-script
  Options +ExecCGI
</Directory>
<Directory /www/xmlserver/htdocs>
  Require all granted
</Directory>
```

Not much to it.

Second Step: Serve the Web Pages

So, at this point we have a server configured, but we don't have any content. We are going to serve up plain HTML and use XML to POST information to the server and receive some information back. We'll dump the files we need into the /www/xmlserver/ htdocs folder (our document root). Here is where to get the files:

The HTML page with the submit forms for testing came from here: *http://65.183.160.36/ Samples/Yips_util/dspfoil.php?afile=/www/zendsvr/htdocs/Samples/Toolkit_HTML/index.html*

The XSL came from here: *http://65.183.160.36/Samples/Yips_util/dspfoil.php?afile=/ www/zendsvr/htdocs/Samples/Toolkit_HTML/DemoXslt.xsl*

I put *both* into the htdocs root, so in order to properly use them, you'll need a tweak or two. In index.html, find the lines (there is one referenced on each <form>) with:

```
<?xml-stylesheet type='text/xsl' href='/Samples/Toolkit_HTML/DemoXslt.xsl'?>
```

and change them to:

```
<?xml-stylesheet type='text/xsl' href='/DemoXslt.xsl'?>
```

And put the DemoXslt.xsl file in the /htdocs folder as well. Remember: all this stuff is case sensitive!

Believe it or not, that is all you need to do. If you walk through the HTML, even if you aren't familiar with HTML, you will see some repeating patterns. So let's analyze them a bit before we run the code on the server.

First, scan down to where the first <form> tag is, and you'll see something like this:

```
<form name="input" action="/cgi-bin/xmlcgi.pgm" method="post">
```

That part of the HTML tag tells the HTML how to send the data to the server. Basically it will be using an HTTP POST (versus GET), and the server "action" that is requested is

/cgi-bin/xmlcgi.pgm. This is where your Apache directives come into play. Go back up and take a quick look at the ScriptAlias directive in the configuration file. You see this:

```
ScriptAlias /cgi-bin/ /QSYS.LIB/XMLSERVICE.LIB/
```

This is the magic! That directive will look for a URL that contains /cgi-bin/ and will take the remaining URL string and pass it to /QSYS.LIB/XMLSERVICE.LIB/. What remained in our POST action after /cgi-bin/? xmlcgi.pgm! So, when the form submits to the server, the server will process the content using program XMLCGI in library XMLSERVICE. Nice! The heavy lifting is done there. What is the content we are passing? That is next.

Without doing a "deep dive" in HTML, I am going to give the simplistic analysis of the remaining content. Now, I know some dedicated Web monkeys are going to roll their eyes as they read this explanation, but we don't need to know the full story on HTML in order to use it. POST is different from GET in that if you analyzed a URL that used GET, you might see something like:

```
http://mydomain.com/myaction?parm1='mydata1'&parm2='mydata2'
```

With a POST, you might see just *http://mydomain.com/myaction*, so you'd be thinking: how do you pass parameters in a post? Well, in 99 percent of the simple cases, the "input" HTML elements are the parameters, so as long as you had two input parameters called parm1 and parm2, the server would evaluate them just like it would "explicit" parameters sent in a GET. So, the remaining HTML elements in our POST will be evaluated as parameters in xmlcgi.pgm and used accordingly. What are those parms? Take a look:

The first five are pretty self-explanatory:

```
<input type="hidden" name="db2" value="*LOCAL">
<input type="hidden" name="uid" value="MYUID">
<input type="hidden" name="pwd" value="MYPWD">
<input type="hidden" name="ipc" value="/tmp/rangerhtmlonly">
<input type="hidden" name="ctl" value="*sbmjob"> db2 - Needed (see note)
```

uid is the user ID for user authentication, and pwd is the user's password.

Note: At this point, I inquired about the DB2 versus REST and why DB2 seems to be required. Again, Tony Cairns from IBM comes to the rescue:

> *"XMLSERVICE uses stored procedures in both REST and DB2 drivers. That is, EVERYTHING goes through DB2 including xmlcgi.rpgle (REST RPG CGI). Essentially XMLSERVICE is really just a very, very, very sophisticated store[d] procedure."*

ipc. This will take a bit of explanation. There are two "modes" of access: 1) private and 2) public. Private is pretty much what we experience in the 5250 world *and* in the Web world when a "session" is used, but the HTTP protocol is stateless: each call to the server is clueless about the previous call unless some method of preserving the "state" of the previous call is used (like a session variable that keeps track of what is going on with the connection to a user). 5250 is stateful: you connect uniquely to the IBM i, and that session/job is yours and only yours, until you sign off. In order to make a REST connection type stateful, a folder is created to store the data. That is why the ipc parameter looks like a path, because it is. A "public" connection is assumed to be a one-off connection to retrieve data, so it makes no attempt to keep track of what the last call was all about. Think of it this way: you are at a bar and ask for a beer, and the bartender slides a beer to you, and you are the only one drinking it until you are done (a "private" beer). A "public" beer ... well, let's not go there. If your connection is public, ipc should be set to *NA. If you want support for public-type connections, then you will need to compile CL program CRTXML3 and use it to create the objects in the XMLSERVICE library. However, that means you will be able to process requests on IBM i with no authentication, which may cause your security folks a lot of angst in dealing with what could be unhappy side-effects of knowing your IBM i is unprotected.

ctl. This is yet another value that is affected by your choice to be public or private. If you are using a private connection, then *sbmjob is what you should use. If the connection is public, then *here is the value to use.

From here on out, you define the payload and the response you anticipate. There are two remaining parameters that will be passed to xmlcgi.pgm:

xmlin. this will contain the XML needed by the service program to "figure out" what you are asking for. Here is an example:

```
<input type="hidden" name="xmlin" value="<?xml version='1.0'?>

<?xml-stylesheet type='text/xsl' href='/Samples/Toolkit_HTML/
DemoXslt.xsl'?>
<script>
<cmd>CHGLIBL LIBL(QTEMP XMLSERVTST) CURLIB(XMLSERVTST)</cmd>
</script>"

>
```

The parameter that is passed is called xmlin. You see it defined as a hidden input element in the form. But it is the "value" passed in that parameter that does the heavy lifting. That value is:

```
"<?xml version='1.0'?>
<?xml-stylesheet type='text/xsl' href='/DemoXslt.xsl'?>
<script>
      <cmd>CHGLIBL LIBL(QTEMP XMLSERVTST) CURLIB(XMLSERVTST)</cmd>
   </script>"
```

The .xsl file referenced is the file that describes how to display an XML document of a given type. It has the "rules" for unpacking the contents of our payload. That file will be passed with every call. But the interesting thing is the stuff between <script></script> tags. You should immediately recognize what this particular call will do: it will call the CHGLIBL (Change Library List) command. Very simple.

The stuff between the script tags can get pretty gnarly, though. What is above is a simple call to run a command. Imagine a call to an RPG program that is passing parameters, lots of them. Things get murky pretty quickly. Here is an example of *just* the value of the xmlin parameter on one such call:

```
<script>
<pgm name='ZZSRV' lib='XMLSERVICE' func='ZZARRAY'>
 <parm comment='search this name'>
  <data var='myName' type='10A'>Ranger</data>
 </parm>
 <parm comment='max allowed return'>
  <data var='myMax' type='10i0'>22</data>
 </parm>
 <parm comment='actual count returned'>
  <data var='myCount' type='10i0' enddo='mycount'>0</data>
 </parm>
 <return>
  <ds var='dcRec_t' dim='999' dou='mycount'>
    <data var='dcMyName' type='10A'>na</data>
    <data var='dcMyJob' type='4096A'>na</data>
    <data var='dcMyRank' type='10i0'>0</data>
    <data var='dcMyPay' type='12p2'>0.0</data>
  </ds>
 </return>
</pgm>
</script>">
```

The program to run is defined along with the library where it is found and, in this particular example, a sub-procedure that is to be run. You can add comments for clarity, and then you define not only the data types but also the data that is passed. As you can see, there is quite a bit of detail to attend to. The really good news here is that the format is more or less a "template" for each call to your program, so you can probably create this content on the fly, programmatically. The RPG that will be called looks like this:

```
D zzarray         PR                 likeds(dcRec_t) dim(ARRAYMAX)
D  myName                    10A
D  myMax                     10i 0
D  myCount                   10i 0
                                                    Continued
```

```
….............

*+++++++++++++++++++++++++++++++++++++++++++++++++++++++++++++
* zzarray: check return array aggregate
*+++++++++++++++++++++++++++++++++++++++++++++++++++++++++++++
P zzarray          B                    export
D zzarray          PI                   likeds(dcRec_t) dim(ARRAYMAX)
D   myName                   10A
D   myMax                    10i 0
D   myCount                  10i 0
 * vars
D i                 S        10i 0 inz(0)
D max               S        10i 0 inz(ARRAYMAX)
D findMe            DS                   likeds(dcRec_t) dim(ARRAYMAX)
 /free
  if myMax <= max;
    max = myMax;
  endif;
  for i = 1 to max;
    findMe(i).dcMyName = %trim(myName) + %char(i);
    if myMax > 10;
      memset(%ADDR(findMe(i).dcMyJob):193:4095); // 'A'
    else;
      findMe(i).dcMyJob  = 'Test 10' + %char(i);
    endif;
    findMe(i).dcMyRank = 10 + i;
    findMe(i).dcMyPay  = 13.42 * i;
    myCount = i;
  endfor;
  return findMe;
 /end-free
P                  E
```

Inbound parameters passed in and an outbound parameter of a data structure!

Here is one more example, with an SQL call this time:

```
<script>
<sql>
<options options='noauto' autocommit='off'/>
</sql>
<sql>
<connect conn='myconn' options='noauto'/>
</sql>
<sql>
<query conn='myconn'>select * from xmlservtst/animal</query>
</sql>
<sql>
<describe desc='col'/>
</sql>
<sql>
<fetch block='all' desc='on'/>
</sql>
<sql>
<free/>
</sql>
</script>
```

The code returns the whole record set. Done!

The last parameter is the xmlout parameter, which defines the size of the data being retrieved. Go big if you are unsure.

So a complete example would be (for a simple command call):

```
<!-- XMLSERVICE call a *CMD CHGLIBL -->
<form name="input" action="/cgi-bin/xmlcgi.pgm" method="post">
<input type="hidden" name="db2" value="*LOCAL">
                                                        Continued
```

```
<input type="hidden" name="uid" value="*NONE">
<input type="hidden" name="pwd" value="*NONE">
<input type="hidden" name="ipc" value="/tmp/rangerhtmlonly">
<input type="hidden" name="ctl" value="*sbmjob">
<input type="hidden" name="xmlin"
value="<?xml version='1.0'?>
<?xml-stylesheet type='text/xsl' href='/Samples/Toolkit_HTML/
DemoXslt.xsl'?>
<script>
<cmd>CHGLIBL LIBL(QTEMP XMLSERVTST) CURLIB(XMLSERVTST)</cmd>
</script>">
<input type="hidden" name="xmlout" value="32768">
<input type="submit" value="call *CMD (CHGLIBL)" />
</form>
```

The <input type="submit"> on an HTML form displays a **Submit** button that will submit the form to the server.

There are XMLSERVICE implementations (aka Toolkits) for PHP, Ruby (PowerRuby), Microsoft .NET, Python, and Node.js. Once you understand the basics, though, you could write an XMLSERVICE implementation for just about any language. Each language chapter of this book deals with the implementation-specific details of the XMLSERVICE toolkit for each language.

5

¡ Object!

We're all familiar with the concept of an object-based operating system like IBM i, but an object-oriented (OO) programming language is foreign to some. Oh, you might have tripped across it in some generic computer science class, but perhaps it was too long ago or you were groggy enough in class that that particular chapter has been forgotten. If so, we are going to take a very brief trip down the orientation road (don't worry, we aren't talking about *that* kind of orientation).

It's probably been a while since you played with Play-Doh unless you have kids or grandkids. Remember how you'd take a chunk of that stuff, flatten it, take a cookie cutter or some kind of mold, and stamp out a Play-Doh object? If so, you were dealing with an OO metaphor. Sure, you could work that stuff with your hands and try to make a flat tree, or person, or dog "freestyle," but being able to grab a mold and stamp out an object shaped like a tree, person, or dog made it that much easier and consistent. Well, in OO programming, that's just what we want to do: crank out consistent objects easily and quickly without cranking out unstable code (or, in some cases, we create consistently unstable code!).

Objects typically have these characteristics:

1. Contain data (sometimes called fields)
   a. Class variables
   b. Instance variables
2. Contain code (called methods or procedures)
   a. Class methods
   b. Instances

The astute reader would recognize that if there are class things and instance things (aka *instantiation*), then there must be some connection between the two. Right you are! Objects typically rely on a property called *inheritance*. Before you get excited about collecting on your inheritance, what we mean in the case of objects is that instances of the class inherit the characteristics of the class, a copy in other words. So unless you want a copy of your aunt's money, inheritance in an object world won't be fungible. It'll get you just a few years in an orange jumpsuit for counterfeiting. The class becomes a "cookie cutter" to stamp out similarly shaped objects.

My first foray into the OO programming world was SmallTalk. I don't know *why* I chose SmallTalk except it sounded cool, and the quick overviews I read made it sound drop-dead simple to use. Instead of simple, I thought I was experiencing some '70s-style flashbacks with mind-bending concepts like polymorphism (illegal in Texas), encapsulation, reflection, abstraction, constructors, and on and on. *Everything* in SmallTalk was an object. Everything! I immediately wrote a couple of RPG programs just to restore my sanity. But the light bulb had turned on, and although I could have turned to LISP (the granddaddy of OO programming), or Python, or C++, or Ruby, I turned instead to Java. I had the good fortune of taking a beginning Java programming class with an instructor who was not only an excellent Java programmer, but someone who could also communicate in real English that I could understand. So here, as I can best describe them, are the necessary basics as I see them.

Classes

These are representations of (usually) real-life objects. Take a bank account, for example. It would typically have an account number, a balance, and some methods for adding money to and removing money from the account. So we could create one of these things, and typically when you create a bank account, you are issued a number and a beginning balance.

```
Account (class)
    variable: Account Number
    variable: balance
    constructor: Account number, beginning balance
    method: deposit (money)
    method: withdraw (money)
    method: display balance (money)
```

We are working with pseudo-code at this point, so the basic description of this class is that it has two properties (data fields). One contains the account number, and one contains the current balance. It also has four methods:

- A constructor—This takes an account number and a beginning balance as parameters. A constructor is a "built-in" method that most objects will have. Basically, it allows for certain values to be passed in and may even trigger other methods during the creation of an instance of the class. You determine what the constructor may do when an instance is created. It may do nothing.
- Deposit—This method adds money to the balance.
- Withdraw—This method removes money from the balance.
- Display balance—This method simply outputs the balance for display.

These types of transactions would be common to any instance of the class Account. When you create a new account for Pete, you might do it by passing in 1234 as the account number and $5 as the beginning balance in the constructor of the new account. If you were to invoke the display balance method on the Pete account, it would return $5.00.

Encapsulation

There are a couple of things to learn about classes. First is *encapsulation*. As you create a class definition, you try to encapsulate the functional pieces into methods rather than update data values directly. Sure, you might be able to update the account balance by just adding the money directly to the balance (balance = balance + money), but for many reasons that I won't go into, it is better to create a method that encapsulates the logic. So yes, when you invoke the "deposit" method in your Account object, the code may well work (balance = balance + money), but you are indirectly accessing the balance rather than directly updating it. Yes, you could walk into the bank, open your wallet, take out the cash, and then have a guard accompany you to the accountant, who would make a note of the amount and then walk outside, take the armored car to the Federal Reserve bank, and stuff it into the giant bank vault directly. Or you could just make a deposit and let the internals of the system handle the rest.

The second thing, of course, is that you created an instance of the original class rather than using the class directly. Certainly, if you wanted to, you could create a brand-new class and store everything in it, but since you'll create millions of these things, why not do that with an Account (new!) command?

Inheritance

So, with encapsulation and instantiation through creating an instance taken care of (more or less), what about inheritance? Inheritance is really a process of saying that you have a model that's close, but it's not exactly what you want. In fact, you have several of these "oh so close!" models that are similar to one another but different from the original model. This is where *subclassing* comes into play. Subclassing means taking an original class and then extending it to include other characteristics.

For example, if you need a credit type of account, it certainly would have an account number and a balance, but it also might have a service charge data field and an interest data field. Since you already have an account with everything you need with the exception of service charges and interest rates, you could say something like: Credit Account is an extension of Account. Inherit everything that Account class has, but add:

```
variable: Service charge
variable: Interest rate
method: Add service charge
method: calculate interest
```

So your class for Credit Account would have this if you could examine it:

```
variable: Account Number
variable: balance
```

```
variable: Service charge
variable: Interest rate
constructor: Account number, beginning balance
method: deposit (money)
method: withdraw (money)
method: display balance (money)
method: Add service charge
method: calculate interest
```

Java uses extend: class CreditAccount extends Account. Ruby uses the < operator: class CreditAccount > Account. Python uses parentheses to denote the base class: class CreditAccount(Account). Get the picture? One class based on another.

Interfaces

With inheritance, you can subclass only one class. But what if you had more than one "template" class that you wanted to inherit? You could create a template that is "less" than a class in that it has no functional methods but basically says you must have this function and that function and this function without really defining what the function must do. Then the class would "implement" those functions with specific code.

Going back to our Account example: you might require that any Account created have an account number as a string value and also have a "deposit" method for getting money into the account, but exactly *how* the deposit is made is left up to the programmer to determine. But you do require that the Account class implements the needed methods. This type of class is typically called an "interface" in that it provides only the barest description of what is needed and leaves the implementation details up to the programmer.

That leads us to the last concept I want to tepidly step into ...

Polymorphism

At the easiest-to-understand level, you can reflect on what adding a "print" method might mean in a few different contexts. Your print() method in an analog world might trigger a line-by-line text output in one environment; a glossy, color page in another environment; a 3D image in another environment; and a Web page in yet another environment. The print() method is polymorphic, outputting completely different things with completely different programming yet invoked with the same call.

Classes can be polymorphic as well. The point is that the class/object/method is manipulated in different ways even though the original call or reference looks nearly identical. That is a *very* simplistic and incomplete description of polymorphism. Even if you don't understand it, no doubt you'll use it without thinking about it at some point in OO programming.

Have Some Class
Finally ...

As we go through each chapter, I'll attempt to point out which of the concepts above we might be dealing with. I say *might* because there are some cases where it just isn't 100 percent clear what concept is being applied.

Generally, seeing this stuff in action is more helpful than just talking about it, and if I were writing about *only one* language, then I could give you comprehensive examples in that language. But since I am writing a multilingual book, I'll give examples in upcoming chapters.

Well, the *programming context* is multilingual; I can speak and write only English, with the exception of *una cerveza por favor* or *Ein bier bitte* or *HIq qIj vItlhutlh vIneHor* (Klingon).

6

Ruby and IBM i

I remember when I first tripped across Ruby. I was looking for an open source report-writing tool and discovered DataVision (*datavision.sourceforge.net*). It was pretty cool for its time (I was using it in early 2003), but my stumbling block was the need to use Ruby to script some of the output. At the time, I thought I was a pretty hot programmer, but my background in RPG III, RPG/400, and BASIC left me ill-prepared for an object-oriented (OO) scripting language like Ruby. I set DataVision aside, and it seems to have faded into the open source diaspora, collecting dust in the vast wasteland that is SourceForge.

But like your Uncle Fred, Ruby has been around a lot longer than you think (some think maybe Fred has been around too long), and it has continued to grow and mature. Ruby got its start in 1993 in response to Yukihiro Matsumoto's need for a "better" scripting language. We're always looking for better, aren't we? And we *can* always do better! So more power to Matz (as he is called) for stepping out into the great unknown of programming language development. His goal for that "better" language was to keep it simple and easy (yeah, right, *every* language seeks that holy grail), so he threw Lisp, SmallTalk, Python, and a bit of Perl into the pot, and the result was Ruby. Lisp brings the simplicity, SmallTalk provides the object-oriented-ness, and Python and Perl sharpen the focus of the language on utility. Matz described Ruby as "a scripting language that was more powerful than Perl, and more object-oriented than Python." He achieved his goal, and eventually the language made its way out of Japan and into the big, wide world of open source around the turn of the century.

The goal of this chapter on Ruby and IBM i is to first ground you in the Ruby language. That won't be easy because Ruby is probably about as different from RPG as an apple is from an orange. They are both fruits, but one must be peeled before eating and they taste very different. We are going to first "peel" Ruby so you can understand how it works. That means a grounding in OO principles. Then we can move on to basic language syntax, access to PASE resources, DB2 for IBM i database access, and then calling RPG programs from Ruby. That's quite a bit to cover. Ready? Let's go!

Every programmer wants to achieve the greatest amount of work in the least amount time and have fun doing it. At least, I hope that's what you're after. The programming world rotates on productivity, and that's what Ruby is designed for. It frees you to produce useful solutions that are easy to write and maintain. Give that some thought for a minute, and then let's take a common construct like a collection of "stuff." An array is basically a listing or grouping of separate but similar things. Very often, you want to access those items individually, and usually you want to do it sequentially. So iterating through these items is something you often do. It would seem logical that a container of these items would "know" what is in "itself" and be able to list those items. Being able to tell the container "list these items" would be a handy feature of the container. Something like this:

My tool bench has these items: hammer, saw, old underwear (yeah—rags), screwdriver, empty cans, vise, pliers. What if the tool bench itself could enumerate and access those items? Maybe something like an each function? So, for each item on the bench, what exactly would the function do? Whatever you told it to do! So we'd end up with a few functions that we often do for the tool bench "collection." Enumerate each item and maybe use a find function (useful for my tool bench). Functions built around that container would maybe look like bench.each and bench.find, where you'd have an operator on the object itself. Ruby ends up looking just like that in many cases because it operates on the *principle of least surprise* (or *astonishment*, in this case), which results in a tidy acronym of POLA. In a POLA world, what you expect to see is what you *do* see.

In the IBM i world, that is not always the way languages and/or commands work. Sometimes it is a POLA opposite. Anyone who made the transition from the S/38 to the AS/400 had to rethink some commands. In many cases, AS/400 commands operated on POLA principles, but not always. And then, once you were in RPG, things were not always so predictable. Take a look at a bit of fun RPG II code:

```
C            RCODE      COMP '0'                    20
C            *IN20      IFEQ '1'
C                       EXFMTSCREEN2
C            AGAIN      COMP 'Y'                     22
C     22                GOTO BEGIN
C     20N22             GOTO END
```

It isn't immediately apparent just what this code does, and it's probably unfair to compare a procedural language to an OO one. I will say that free-format RPG is much more coherent to me, and is easier to transition to, than the RPG II above. Then again, RPG II *is* more readable than assembly language (which I was completely spared from ever having to learn). Bottom line: the principle behind Ruby is POLA, and it does a pretty good job. In fact, it does such a good job that initial forays into the language can be disorienting.

Moving to a predictable environment from an unpredictable one can be just as disorienting as the opposite approach. When I moved to Salt Lake City from Chicago, the grid-style layout of the streets in Salt Lake left me dumbfounded until I adapted to the Salt Lake way of navigating. After 20 years, you could plop me down anywhere in the Salt Lake valley and I could find my way home. Moving from that rigid structure to the rambling roads of San Antonio, I had to turn on my GPS to find my way to the next block. Plop me down a few miles from home in San Antonio, and I'd be lost without a GPS. But I have learned new rules and now regularly ignore my GPS and I am fine ("Oh, look, what is an ocean doing so close to San Antonio?"). Bottom line: you can learn this stuff. Ruby operates on POLA. POLA is good!

So, with that brief primer and the established principle of POLA, let's take a look at some Ruby basics just to get started.

Installation

You will most likely want to have some kind of command line into the world of Ruby, so we have a couple of ways we can go. If you are a Windows, Linux, or Mac person, you can find pretty much all you need at the *https://www.ruby-lang.org* site. Even if you plan to install PowerRuby on IBM i (which you will find here: *https://powerruby.com*), you'll probably still want to have something local so you don't have to lug that Power Systems box around with you. One of the cool features of open source on IBM i is that, except for RPG-based projects, you can write, compile, test, and deploy projects wherever you want initially. When you're ready, you can deploy to IBM i and test again in that environment. Basically, you can write code whenever and wherever you want. I find that very productive (and a little invasive in my life).

I won't go into details on how to install Ruby. There are plenty of tutorials on how to do that (and they are simple), so go ahead and install Ruby on both your development workstation and IBM i (if you have that freedom). The following examples will run anywhere.

IDEs and irb

We haven't talked about IDEs for Ruby. Frankly, an IDE for Ruby would be like an IDE for CL: I guess it would be cool for syntax checking, but it's overkill for basically a text editor. In fact, that's really all you need: a text editor. Notepad, Notepad++, WordPad, LaunchPad (I just made that up)—any kind of pad will do (like back in the 1960s). I use the Sublime Text editor for a couple of reasons: it's cheap, and I can run the code directly within the editor. There are others, so find one that fits like that comfy 10-year-old shirt you keep in the back of your closet and keep it easy. No reason to get hung up on text editor versus IDE wars.

You have another option for testing small snippets of code or just trying a few lines to get the hang of something: a REPL. Rather than some alter-ego clone, a REPL is a read-eval-print loop terminal, and it can really come in handy when you are just getting started. You usually get a REPL by just invoking the executable. In Ruby, you use the irb (Interactive RuBy) command. It will look like Figure 6.1 if you are a Windows user and have installed Ruby.

Figure 6.1: The Ruby irb *command*

There isn't any console support in the CMD window in Windows, so you'll see that message on the startup of irb.

Here's a really simple "Hello World" example (dang, I really didn't want to go there, but we always start with a "Hello World" example), as shown in Figure 6.2.

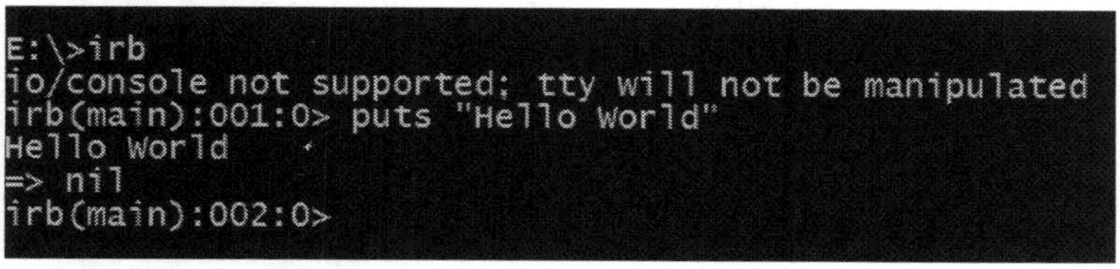

Figure 6.2: Hello World example

The command entry point here is after the line number 001:0 and the greater-than sign (>). And what's with the =>nil? Well, we asked Ruby to output the string "Hello World" (that is what puts does), and the puts command returns nothing, nada, zilch. Hence, to be different and a little British, it returns "nil." Nothing to worry about.

We could just keep slamming out commands in irb, but it can get a bit tedious if we are trying to write a complete script. You can end a line with a semicolon (;) to indicate that there is more to come, or if you are in a do block, you can code your little heart out until you end it. But a text editor will make things easier in the long run.

A REPL is cool because you can immediately see the results of your programming, but if you have several lines of code, it can get a little tedious, as you can see in Figure 6.3.

```
irb(main):015:0> puts "Hello you";
irb(main):016:0* puts "Hello me";
irb(main):017:0* puts "Hello everybody";
irb(main):018:0* puts "Hello world"
Hello you
Hello me
Hello everybody
Hello world
=> nil
irb(main):019:0>
```

Figure 6.3: Code in a REPL

It might just be easier to stuff the whole thing into a text file. That way, if you fat-finger a couple of lines, you won't have to laboriously retrieve and edit each line at a time. You can hack the file and be done with it.

Figure 6.4 shows a snippet of code I knocked out in UltraEdit (I could have used any other editor). It does what I just tediously typed out in irb (except you didn't see all the correcting going on).

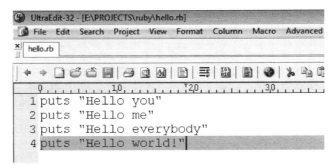

Figure 6.4: The same code in an editor

Going to the command line and typing ruby and the filename will run the script:

```
bash-4.2$ ruby sayhello.rb
Hello you
Hello me
Hello everybody
Hello world
```

But, Ruby really doesn't give a rip about the .rb file extension. You can run Ruby against any file that has valid Ruby commands in it, like this:

```
bash-4.2$ ruby hello.pete
Hello you
Hello me
Hello everybody
Hello world!
```

The convention is to use .rb at the end because, in most cases, you have associated the .rb extension with the Ruby binary (in Windows) and a shebang (#!) directive to point to the correct executable (in PASE), and that combination will "know" how to run the script:

```
#!/usr/bin/env ruby
puts "Hello you"
puts "Hello me"
puts "Hello everybody"
puts "Hello world"
```

But really, as long as you point Ruby to a file with valid syntax, no problemo! Ruby will parse and execute the script.

What if your syntax *is* problematic? Then what? Let's make a very subtle (and common) mistake and see what happens. First, the file contents:

```
puts "Hello you"
puts "Hello me"
Puts "Hello everybody"
puts "Hello world"
```

Then run it:

```
bash-4.2$ ruby sayhello.rb
Hello you
Hello me
sayhello.rb:3:in '<main>': undefined method 'Puts' for main:Object (No-
MethodError)
```

What the heck? Undefined method 'Puts'? We have been "putting" all day. What's up? Well, Ruby is case-sensitive. Welcome to *that* world! A host of languages are sensitive to case, and Ruby is one of them. In this case, our script happily executed each line until it got to line three, which had 'Puts' instead of 'puts', and Ruby barfed. Some text editors that have syntax checking can catch this kind of thing (which is a good thing). Distinguishing between 'Puts' and 'puts' is pretty easy, but most text editors, even with highlighting and syntax checking, won't always give you the correct feedback all the time.

Getting tired of that Windows command window? Well, on the IBM i, we can do something pretty similar. You *could* start by going to the 5250 command line and starting QSH or QSHELL, but STRQSH, QSH, and QSHELL start a PASE (UNIX)-like environment shell that really wasn't designed to run AIX programs (so don't bother). You could also run QP2TERM, which is a shell that *is* a more AIX (PASE)-friendly environment. Figures 6.5 and 6.6 offer a quick look at some of the results of using the two shells and invoking Ruby.

```
                         QSH Command Entry

 $
> ruby -v
 [FATAL] Failed to create timer thread: Resource temporarily unavailable
 $
```

Figure 6.5: QSHELL invoking Ruby

Yikes! Probably not a good idea to continue.

```
                         /QOpenSys/usr/bin/-sh

 $
> ruby -v
 ruby 2.1.9p490 (2016-03-30 revision 54437) [powerpc-aix6.1]
 $
```

Figure 6.6: QP2TERM invoking Ruby

That's more like it!

If we copy a Ruby script file over to the IFS and run it, we get the same results as we did in Windows, as shown in Figure 6.7.

```
                                    /QOpenSys/usr/bin/-sh

 $
> ruby hello.pete
  Hello you
  Hello me
  Hello everybody
  Hello world!
 $
```

Figure 6.7: Running Ruby from the IFS

An easier way, IMHO, is to use a TTY terminal emulator like PuTTY and use Secure Shell (SSH) to connect to your IBM i. You''ll have all of the functionality of QP2TERM without the overhead of also running a 5250 emulator (although TTY is basically a terminal emulator).

I use PuTTY for my access to PASE, but there are plenty of free alternatives. Figure 6.8 shows what the script in Figure 6.7 looks like in PuTTY (and BASH).

```
10.0.10.200 - PuTTY

login as: pete
pete@10.0.10.200's password:
$ bash
bash-4.2$ ruby hello.pete
Hello you
Hello me
Hello everybody
Hello world!
bash-4.2$
```

Figure 6.8: Using PuTTy and BASH

Boringly similar to all the other scripts and REPL examples we have looked at, isn't it?

So that's a very basic first step toward using a REPL like irb and executing scripts at the command line. So far, it's pretty easy.

Next, we need to take a look at a few more programming constructs before stepping back to examine classes and modules.

Most of the Ruby language constructs follow a predictable pattern that we, as programmers, are familiar with. It is the implementation of those constructs that can make the "getting started" step a bumpy ride. So let's get on the horse and ride!

Language Basics

I don't plan to spend a lot of time in the minutiae of the Ruby language. The goal of this book is to give you enough to go on to get started. Proficiency won't be the end result. And although Ruby is based on POLA, there is enough "surprise!" in the way things work that it is worthwhile to go over some of the basic things and at least point out where I got either derailed or stumped. Sometimes, Grasshopper, all you need is a little enlightenment!

Variables

Unlike RPG and more like JavaScript (if you are familiar with it), Ruby is a dynamically typed language. That is, you don't have to declare a type when you declare a variable.

You could assign a variable this way:

```
the_meaning_of_life = 42
```

If you do, Ruby will see the variable as a number (Fixnum class, actually). Later, you could assign the same variable to a different type:

```
the_meaning_of_life = 'Money, fame and fortune'
```

Ruby won't even blink. If you happened to capitalize the first character of the variable, Ruby will define it as a constant. And, although you *can* change the value of a constant, Ruby *will* complain about it with a warning about the change.

```
bash-4.2$ irb
irb(main):001:0> the_meaning_of_life = 42
```
Continued

```
=> 42
irb(main):002:0> the_meaning_of_life = 'Money, fame and fortune'
=> "Money, fame and fortune"
## Note no complaint about the change.....
irb(main):003:0> The_meaning_of_life = 42
=> 42
irb(main):004:0> The_meaning_of_life = 'Money, fame and fortune'
(irb):4: warning: already initialized constant The_meaning_of_life
(irb):3: warning: previous definition of The_meaning_of_life was here
=> "Money, fame and fortune"
```

Scope

We also have variables that can be of local, global, class, or instance scope.

Local scope is pretty much what you would expect, and global variables are pretty much the same in Ruby as in other languages. Each variable will have a scope that it is declared in based on its location in the code.

You probably have not come across class and instance variables either because, well, RPG isn't object-oriented, so the concepts of classes and instances of classes are not part of your nomenclature in RPG. From chapter 5, you should have a rough idea of what a class and an instance of a class would be. Very quickly, in most cases a class represents a template or a "mold" of what an object should look like from the standpoint of the design of variables and function. It's a prototype of what the object would look like if you created one. So a class variable would be a variable that would hold a value across instances of that class. This could come in handy if you are creating many instances of a class and want an aggregate count or total across all instances of that class. An instance variable would be, ahem, a variable that is unique to only that instance of the class. No mystery. But the declaration of each of the variables has some convention to it:

- Local variables: start with a lowercase letter or an underscore "_"
- Global variables: start with a $ sign
- Class variables: start with a double "at" sign: @@
- Instance variables: start with a single "at" sign: @

The best way to demonstrate how each of these works is to demonstrate them (!).

```
### Start with a global that will persist for the session
$aGlobalVariable = 5

## Then create a class to demonstrate class and instance differences

class Demo
## class Variable
@@classVariable = 0

        ## We need to initialize the variable or else it will be nil when
        ## we add it to itself in the add_me method. Initialization will
        ## happen when we invoke "New" on the class to create the
        ## instance

        def initialize()
            @instanceVariable = 0
        end

        ## a simple function to output these variables
        def add_me()

            @@classVariable += 1  # increment the class variable
            @instanceVariable += 1 # increment the instance variable
            output_class_var()
            puts "Global total is now #$aGlobalVariable"
            puts "My instance variable is now #@instanceVariable"
            puts " "
        end
        def add_me_twice()
            ## Run this guy to see what happens to a global variable
            $aGlobalVariable+=1
            add_me
        end
```
Continued

```
        def output_class_var
                puts "Class total is now #@@classVariable"
        end
end

#  Create the class instances (objects), which will initialize
#  the instance variable
i1 = Demo.new
i2 = Demo.new

# invoke the methods
i1.add_me()
i2.add_me()
i2.add_me_twice()
i3 = Demo.new
i3.output_class_var()
```

The output will be this:

```
Class total is now 1
Global total is now 5
My instance variable is now 1

Class total is now 2
Global total is now 5
My instance variable is now 1

Class total is now 3
Global total is now 6
My instance variable is now 2

Class total is now 3
```

The first invocation is predictable. Those values were set in the instance. But in the next invocation of add_me in a *different* instance of the class, we see the magic start to happen.

Even though i2 knows nothing about i1 and what it is doing, it is affected by the method that updates the global variable. And if we create a new object instance *after* the class variable has been updated, we get the new total along with it, as you can see when i3 invokes the output_class_var method.

Trying to keep track of the variables and their scope can be a challenge, but what I like here is that we can use the underscore (_), dollar sign ($), at sign (@), and double at signs (@@) as part of the variable name to help us keep track of what is what. Normally, I would have to resort to using special naming conventions to remind me of the scope. This way, I can know exactly what the scope is by the name used.

Built-in Functions

At the simplest level, there are math functions:

```
irb(main):005:0> 1+1
=> 2
```

Fortunately, it can also do math correctly: 1 + 1 is 2.

Ruby math follows the correct order of precedence rule rather than the "calculator" (sequence) rules.

```
irb(main):006:0> 20-10*10
=> -80
```

Multiplication has a higher order of precedence than subtraction. And you can "force" calculations into a higher precedence by using parentheses:

```
irb(main):007:0> (20-10)*10
=> 100
```

Beyond the "primitive" math functions of add, subtract, multiply, and divide are a whole host of math functions found in the Math module, such as square root (sqrt).

```
irb(main):008:0> Math.sqrt(25)
=> 5.0
```

Or you could just include the Math module and then execute the functions directly:

```
irb(main):009:0> include Math
=> Object
irb(main):010:0> sqrt(25)
=> 5.0
```

OK. We have seen a couple of things here. We've seen the native arithmetic functions and those contributed by the Math modules (we'll be jumping into modules and classes shortly). We still have a few more commonly used features of the Ruby language that are worth exploring.

Containers

Back to the workbench that contained many items, including my underwear.

Arrays and hashes are typical containers. The RPG language has arrays, but hashes are a bit different. Let's start with arrays. You can define them with literals using brackets ([]) or by declaring an object type: Array.

The elements do not have to all be the same type. You can mix and match:

```
irb(main):011:0> a = [123,'cat','bird',6,'dog']
=> [123, "cat", "bird", 6, "dog"]
irb(main):012:0> puts a[3]
6
```

So we have an array of four items, strings, and numbers and have assigned them to the variable a. From that context, we know we have an array type. Let's check that:

```
irb(main):013:0> a.class
=> Array
```

It confirms what we already know.

We can also create a new array object:

```
irb(main):014:0> b = Array.new()
=> []
```

You can assign values:

```
irb(main):015:0> b[0]=123
=> 123
irb(main):016:0> b[1]='cat'
=> "cat"
irb(main):017:0> b[2]='bird'
=> "bird"
irb(main):018:0> b[3]=6
=> 6
irb(main):019:0> b[4]='dog'
=> "dog"
```

And you can output those arrays. More importantly, you can iterate through them, which is what you commonly do with arrays. Here is an example of iterating through an array:

```
irb(main):020:0> b.each{|i| puts i}
123
cat
bird
6
dog
=> [123, "cat", "bird", 6, "dog"]
```

What might blow your mind a bit is the {|i| puts i} part. I know it did for me the first time I saw the syntax. What you are seeing is a "block," which is a way of defining an anonymous function or closure. In RPG, we generally define each of the functions we'll call in the RPG program. In Ruby (and not just Ruby, but several other languages, such as JavaScript and Python), you can execute a function without naming it. So, in the example above, b, an array, has an each method that, when invoked, iterates through the array passing "each" element. Passing "each" to what? Passing to a block function, in this case. The function takes a parameter (| |), and then the rest of the function block defines what to do with that parameter puts i. A single-line function is easily represented with the { | | } syntax. But if you have a complex block, you can use the do ... end syntax, which basically defines what to "do" between do and end.

On the face of it, it's pretty simple, but you don't often see a simple block like this. Very often, blocks are passed to methods, and then things get a *little* more wiggy.

Take a look at something like this:

```
def say_stuff

yield ("Pete", "ruby")

end

say_stuff do |name, lang|

puts "#{name} loves to program #{lang}"

end
```

We have a method called say_stuff, which takes no parameters and has a yield method that is passing two parameters.

Below that, we have a call to the say_stuff method, which is passing a block. So what is going on here? Let's start with yield. Yield basically says, "Stop here and call whatever was passed in as a block." Frankly, at this point, the POLA (Principle of Least Astonishment) is completely broken IMHO because my head exploded the first time I tried to puzzle out the code. Ruby allows a block to be passed to any method, even if it isn't used. But, if there *is* a yield, then you *have to* pass it a block or it will raise an exception. (Well, almost. You can use the block_given? method to test to see whether a block was passed and then act accordingly.)

The other thing that strikes me as bass-ackwards in this approach is that most of the magic is in the block that is called rather than the method. So things take a while to sink in. And here is the result:

```
bash-4.2$ ruby block_stuff.rb
Pete loves to program ruby
```

So, we invoke the say_stuff method, passing in our block (the stuff between the do and end). We run line number 2, which yields to the block passed in, passing in the two parameters that the block uses. The function in the block runs, and then the function returns, and then the method returns. Done.

You see plenty of this in Ruby, so get used to it. The Internet has many examples of blocks and methods. This example barely scrapes the surface. But my goal is to get you familiar with the language and expose you to Ruby stuff so your head stays intact, not teach you everything you need to know.

Hashes

Our little trip down the array path got us diverted on to blocks. But blocks are used extensively with arrays because normally you are iterating through the array to do something with each value in the array or at least examine each value. Hashes are similar to arrays. There really isn't an equivalent data type in RPG that I can think of (a data structure, maybe). But, in principle, hashes are arrays of name-value or key-value pairs, and sometimes key:value or name:value. And the advantage to the hash design is that basically anything can be the key, so it becomes a great way to store stuff with arbitrary keys and values. In an array, your values are stored in sequential buckets. In a hash, they could be stored anywhere; you have to find it by key. That is also a disadvantage of hashes: they have no order like an array would have, so finding the value by key can be slow.

But a key-value pair is highly flexible. In fact, when we look at Rails and a few other Web technologies later on, the key-value pair will raise its head in the form of JSON. So, this isn't just an intellectual exercise; there is some goodness here!

To create a hash, you can do it two ways (just like arrays). You can use literals or use Object.new to create a "new" object of "type." Option #1 will let us use symbols and "rocket" nomenclature to assign key-value pairs:

```
h = {'cat'=>'unlikeable','dog'=>'best friend','horse'=>'giddy
up','pig'=>'squeal!'}
```

And as a side note, you can use symbols for keys as well:

```
h = {:cat=>'unfriendly',:dog=>'best friend',:horse=>'giddy
up',:pig=>'squeal'}
```

Option 2 is to invoke the new method on a hash object:

```
creatures = Hash.new
```

And then assign the key-value pairs:

```
creatures['cat']='unlikeable'
creatures['dog']='best friend'
creatures['horse']='giddy up'
creatures['pig']='squeal!'
```

How to access the values? Refer to the key, and the value will be returned. This is how to iterate though the hashes:

```
creatures = Hash.new
creatures['cat']='unlikeable'
```

Continued

```
creatures['dog']='best friend'
creatures['horse']='giddy up'
creatures['pig']='squeal!'

creatures.each {|creature,appeal| puts "#{creature} is #{appeal}" }
```

The result of the above code would be this:

```
cat is unlikeable
dog is best friend
horse is giddy up
pig is squeal!
```

Really it just comes down to referencing the key to return the value:

```
puts creatures['cat'] would output "unlikeable".
```

When it comes to hashes, if you can keep the concept of key-value pair in your head, you'll do fine.

With simple syntax, working with hashes is a breeze, and in Ruby (and Rails in particular), you'll use a lot of them.

Program Structure in Ruby

I got us started right away in using irb and writing and testing code because, well, we are programmers and that is what we like to do (well, that and watch old *Star Trek* episodes). But I didn't really spend much time talking about how best to structure and use your Ruby code. In some respects, there isn't a whole lot that is new here if you have been writing modular code and perhaps using free-format RPG. I mention that not because this book is written only for cool programmers who write in a modular way and use RPG /free but because if you are already in that mode of writing code, your thinking about program structure has probably changed. Originally, RPG was pretty linear, so we thought in a linear way, and our code followed. My first exposure to a mega-monolithic RPG program (pushing that 10,000-line limit) was a payroll-processing routine. It was a monster! One record in, and 9,999 lines later, one record out. In order to work around the limit on the number of lines, we wrote a bunch a pre-processing routines that output to temporary files so the next process could take over. Debugging a problem with a payroll check was killer.

If you are writing service programs now, using a more modular design, those kinds of barriers and bottlenecks aren't as challenging, and you probably have already started thinking about breaking your code into logically functional units. Nice! This should be an easy section for you to handle! The beauty of OO programming is that you can think more logically about structure. Think in terms of objects communicating by passing around "messages" and data: run this, use that, send me this—all things that you do in your daily life and that you can use conceptually to structure your code. That is where we are heading. It's a new, modular way of structuring your code (or maybe not so new if you already "think modular").

Modules

I have already mentioned classes, and we can see the value of classes in that entire realms of behavior can be encapsulated in a class, and then any other class can inherit from that class, or we can create instances of the class and even modify those instances to fine tune and add behaviors. But what if we had functionality that we needed across different classes? For example, maybe several of our classes need to connect to a database, and each class needs the same set of database connection functions. We *could* just write the same code over and over in each class. Or we could try to identify the common functions in each class, build a class based on that common set of functions, and then modify the instances of the classes.

There are probably many ways to approach a solution, but I think a solid approach would be to create classes when a "standard" object is needed. That object will have several instances, and each instance, although sharing similar behaviors, may have unique characteristics that will create a unique instance. If you need an identical set of functions that could be applied to many classes, then a "module" will be your friend.

Modules are units of code that provide a standard set of functionality when implemented. Unlike classes, you cannot create an instance of a module. Modules are included by using a highly complex directive called include. (OK, not that complex; POLA lives [as does

Frodo]!) By "including" a module in a class, the class as well as the instances of the class have access to the functions in the module. Let's take a look:

```ruby
module Say_hi

        def speak_en
                sayit = "Hi!"
                #puts sayit
        end
end

class Talker
include Say_hi  ## Include the above module

        def speak_es
                sayit = "Hola!"
                #puts sayit
        end
end

speak = Talker.new  ## create instance
puts speak.speak_en
puts speak.speak_es

yell = Talker.new   ## create instance
puts yell.speak_en.upcase
puts yell.speak_es.upcase

whisper = Talker.new   ## create instance
puts whisper.speak_en.downcase
puts whisper.speak_es.downcase
```

A few cool things are going on here. First, our module has a method called speak_en, and when we include that module that has that method in our class, we can see that an instance of the class will also include that module. This is a powerful concept that, if you can keep it front and center as you develop a solution, will help you modularize your code. The biggest advantage is that if you have to change the code across classes and the code resides in a module, you can tweak the module so that all the classes that contain the module will execute the new code in the module. Trying to figure out when to create a module and when to encapsulate code in a class is the tricky part. No hard and fast rules apply. Just common sense and experience. But, if you find yourself repeating the same code snippet over and over, you might just have a good candidate for a module.

You may also notice that nothing in either of the two functions was told to "return" anything, yet we still got output. How's that? In Ruby, a function will return the value the last executed expression evaluates. You can explicitly code a return statement if you need to return earlier in the function, but in most cases just coding for the last executed statement, wherever it appears in your code, early or late, is all you need to do.

So here is the output of our Talker class and Say_hi module:

```
Hi!
Hola!
HI!
HOLA!
hi!
hola!
```

Modules are also known as "mix-ins" because they mix code into your classes. The best way to "mix in" module code is to store it in a file and then reference it in your class using the filename. And the best way to utilize classes is to store them in a file and then reference them when you need them. And then, if you want to run some Ruby code on a regular basis, it is best to store *that* in a file as well.

If we were to take the code above and break it into its logically separate parts, we'd end up with three files: one that contains our module, one that contains our class, and one that contains our Ruby script to run all that code. So let's do that.

Start with the module:

```
say_hi.rb

module Say_hi
        def speak_en
                sayit = "Hi!"
                #puts sayit
        end
end

talker.rb

require "./say_hi" # Include our file which contains our Module
class Talker
include Say_hi      # Include the Module from the file

        def speak_es
                sayit = "Hola!"
                #puts sayit
        end
end

talker_demo.rb

require "./talker.rb"

speak = Talker.new
puts speak.speak_en
puts speak.speak_es

yell = Talker.new
puts yell.speak_en.upcase
puts yell.speak_es.upcase

whisper = Talker.new
puts whisper.speak_en.downcase
puts whisper.speak_es.downcase
```

Again, we had our module containing the functions in one file. Then we created a class that used the module, so we referenced it by both "requiring" the file containing it and then "including" the module by name. You will also see load used in the same way require is used. Load will load the file every time the module is referenced. Require loads the file only once, when instantiated. When we then use the class in our Ruby script, we again use the require option (or we could use load). Filenames are given in quotes, and an interesting side note is that Ruby doesn't have to use only Ruby files in require or load. Depending upon your solution, you may be using an .so file or a .dll file to take advantage of native functionality. So Ruby will search for a file that matches your "bare" filename and attempt to load it. Just FYI: occasionally, there can be a surprise in referencing a file and getting some weird error in return, so check the path. There might be a file with the same name FUBARing your code.

With our code nicely modularized, we can just run the Ruby script file (talker_demo.rb) directly:

```
E:\examples>talker_demo.rb
Hi!
Hola!
HI!
HOLA!
hi!
hola!
```

Again, in this particular situation, the .rb extension was associated with the Ruby executable in Windows. Back over on IBM i (doncha love how you can move between Windows, Linux, and IBM i for testing and development?), you need to add one additional line to your Ruby script in order to run it by just typing in the filename. Add this as the very first line at the top of the script:

```
#!/usr/bin/env ruby
```

Shebang! The #! with the /usr/bin/env reference followed by ruby tells our scripting shell (Bash, in this case) to run this file in a Ruby environment. So, if the file is marked as "executable" (and if you copy it from Windows to the IFS, it probably will be marked that way), then when you type in the filename at the command line in Bash, it already knows it is an executable file and just needs to be told "how" to execute it. If you leave out the shebang directive at the top of the file, Bash will do its best to execute the file as a Bash script, and the results ..., well, they ain't pretty!

Control Flow in Ruby

We already charged down this path before with iterating through an array and a hash using the each method, but we need to take a quick look at how code can be conditionally executed. The if conditional is a familiar place to start since just about every programmer and language use it.

Start simply:

```
if condition
   # code here, executed if condition is true
end
```

As with any program, the conditional blocks can be any size and can include any number of instructions. It can include other if ... end blocks. We can also go the one-liner route:

```
if x > y then puts x end
```

Slightly more compact is using the semicolon (;) to mimic line endings:

```
if x > y; puts x; end
```

GAHHH! Sometimes terseness isn't helpful. I am a traditional sort of geek and would probably write it this way:

```
if x > y
  puts x
end
```

Whatever floats your boat.

Sometimes you need additional branching options, and although you could do a long nested mess of if ... ends, you could also use else and elsif (yeah, that missing "e" in elsif is going to drive you nuts).

You can provide an else branch in your if statement:

```
if condition
  # code executed if condition is true
else
  # code executed if condition is false
end
```

You can also use an elsif keyword. elsif lets you "cascade" your conditional logic to more levels than you can using just if and else:

```
if condition1
  # code executed if condition1 is true
elsif condition2
  # code executed if condition1 is false
  # and condition2 is true
elsif condition3
  # code executed if neither condition1
  # nor condition2 is true, but condition3 is true
end
```

You can have as many elsif clauses in a given if statement as you want. The code segment corresponding to the first successful if or elsif is executed, and the rest of the statement is ignored:

```
print "Enter an integer: "
n = gets.to_i
```
Continued

```
if n > 0
  puts "Your number is positive."
elsif n < 0
  puts "Your number is negative."
else
  puts "Your number is zero."
end
```

Hmm. I introduced a couple of new concepts here as well. Note the following:

```
print "Enter an integer: "
n = gets.to_i
```

We use print rather than puts because puts (put string) adds a new line after the output. print does not. Where that comes in handy is in a command "prompt" line like above, where waiting for some input just logically follows the prompt. So, up above, the "Enter an integer:" is immediately followed by a gets (yeah, that is "get string"), which is what terminals typically capture when you are typing stuff into a shell: it's text! You need to take that string and convert it to an integer with the to_i method. If you had an integer and wanted to make it into a string, you would use ... you guessed it: the to_s method, as in 101.to_s => "101".

So far we have looked at positive conditionals ("if true then do ..."), but there are also negative conditionals, such as "if !(true) then ..." and "unless true then ...". That is a little different. If you have written JavaScript code, then the negation symbol (!) might be familiar to you. But the unless keyword is pretty foreign and, thankfully, not often used. However, unless can make things more readable. Take a look at the following examples.

One way is to use the not keyword:

```
if not (x == y)
```

You can also use the negating ! (exclamation point, or bang) operator:

```
if !(x == y)
```

Both of these examples use parentheses to set apart the expression being tested. In the first example, you can do this:

```
if not x == y
```

However, you can't omit parentheses in the second example because the negating ! operator binds more tightly (precedence) than the not keyword. In other words, consider what happens if you do this:

```
if !x == y
```

You're really, in effect, comparing the negation of *x* with *y*:

```
if (!x) == y
```

So now to an example that uses unless:

```
unless x == y
```

It's not immediately evident, but it is the same as this:

```
if not x == y
```

The if, else, elsif, unless, and end conditionals can get pretty messy, so I highly recommend that you use indentation to make the code more readable. The nested code can be pretty hard to read:

```
if x > 50
if x > 100
puts "Big number"
else
puts "Medium number"
end
end
```

The code below looks "more better" to me.

```
if x > 50
  if x > 100
    puts "Big number"
  else
    puts "Medium number"
  end
end
```

My guess is that you are hanging in there with these concepts because, well, you probably use them in RPG every day. The unless keyword and the negation symbol (!), to some extent, are probably new to you.

Assignments and conditionals and get a little hard to track if you are not familiar with the equality symbol (==). In RPG, we might evaluate and branch conditionally on something like this:

```
x=2
if x = 1
        puts "Made it through"
        puts x
end
```

Logically, you would think that this code would output nothing, nada, zilch because *x* was
assigned a value of 2 and we only execute the code if the value of *x* is 1. Right? Wrong!
What we did in actuality is revealed when we run the code:

```
irb(main):031:0> if x=1
irb(main):032:1> puts "Made it through"
irb(main):033:1> puts x
irb(main):034:1> end
(irb):31: warning: found = in conditional, should be ==
Made it through
1
=> nil
```

Our nifty program generated the output Made it through, and the value of x is 1!

Looking at the output and reading the warning message, you do a quick dope slap on
the forehead: "I *assigned* the value 1 to x rather than *evaluated* the value of x!" Aye, yi,
yi! My forehead has a well-defined handprint because of *just* this error. Repeat after me:
"Assign with '=' and evaluate with '==' ".

With that slight tweak and a bit more code to clearly express the issue:

```
irb(main):036:0> if x==1
irb(main):037:1> puts "Dope slap!"
irb(main):038:1> else
irb(main):039:1* puts "The value is #{x}"
irb(main):040:1> end
The value is 2
```

Whew! One less dent in the head.

Moving on, let's "case" the joint.

Using Case

Case is a helpful keyword because it can reduce the complexity when multiple evaluations will be happening in a block of code but only a single result will be returned. This would be similar to the Select- EndSL in RPG. Basically, the code looks for a matching condition when ..., like this:

```
print "Enter your name and I'll guess ";
answer = gets.chomp;
print "Is it Pete? <press enter>";
gets;
case answer
when "Pete"
  puts "See, I was right"
  exit
when "Bob"
  puts "Well, Bob is an OK name"
else
  puts "Hmmm...I wouldn't have guessed your name was #{answer}"
end
```

This is a simple program with a couple of new things. First, you'll notice that we are using the chomp method on gets. What chomp does is remove the newline character from the end of the string that is entered. Although not always necessary, chomp can ensure that all you are getting from the "prompt" is the string of characters you are expecting. Second, you can see the case syntax used here. Basically, it evaluates the variable and looks for a match in each when statement. This can be very flexible because, as you might remember, Ruby is an untyped language. So you could write something like this:

```
print "Enter something ";
a = gets.chomp;
a = Float(a) rescue a;
case a
when 1..5
                                                        Continued
```

```
   "It's between 1 and 5"
when 42
   "It's the meaning of life!"
when String
   "You passed a string"
else
   "You gave me #{a} -- I have no idea what to do with that."
end
```

There's something new here as well: rescue. We have spent no time looking at error handling, so there you go! Rescue is basically a way of catching errors. We'll do no deep dive here; I'll just give a quick and dirty explanation of error handling in Ruby.

A Brief Aside into Error Handling

In our example above, we really don't know what the user will enter. If we expect a number, inevitably the user will enter a string and vice versa. Since everything entered at the command line and returned by gets will be a string, we may need a way to intelligently convert one data type to another. So, in this example, I attempt to convert the string returned from gets to a Float (floating point decimal). That will work great if a number is entered, but it will raise an error and fall over if it is anything else.

We can actually see what the exception is if we capture it and examine a couple of properties. Let's rework the example and see what we get:

```
print "Enter something ";
a = gets.chomp;
begin;
   a = Float(a);
   rescue Exception => e;
   puts e.message;
end;
case a
when 1..5
```

Continued

```
    "It's between 1 and 5"
when 42
    "It's the meaning of life!"
when String
    "You passed a string"
else
    "You gave me #{a} -- I have no idea what to do with that."
end
```

This is a wee bit more verbose because now we need to catch and process the error that is raised, if any. In this case, if we entered two as the value, then we would see both the exception and the output "You passed a string", like this:

```
Enter something two
invalid value for Float(): "two"
=> "You passed a string"
```

So with that brief primer on case statements and error handling, let's move on to some other stuff that I think you'll run into early on in your Ruby programming foray: file, I/O, and system operations.

File, I/O, and System Operations

My guess is that, at some point in time, you'll have to interact with more than just variables and parameters. You'll need to store, retrieve, and update data, which is typically called a CRUD operation (Create, Read, Update, and Delete) when accessing a database, or you might just need to read the contents of a text file. CRUD typically has a database I/O focus, whereas accessing a text file is more along the lines of system operations.

We'll look at both, but I am going to start with accessing a file from the IFS (or something similar), and we may wait for database I/O until we jump into the Rails portion of the book.

Ruby would have knowledge of local file system files, but we'll need something beefier in order to open up files and data in the IBM i native world. So let's first look at just accessing a file in the IFS, which Ruby has no problem with.

A Brief Aside into I/O

We have actually already been in the I/O arena because we have been using a REPL (irb) as well as some Ruby files. In each case, the data and the execution of the program had to come from somewhere.

In a command-line (REPL) program, two things exist in the environment that help with I/O. First, three constants give us access to I/O: STDIN, STDOUT, and STDERR. These are I/O objects dedicated to the proposition that all data should read and write (good skills to have if you want a job). The job is to take input (read through STDIN) and produce output (write—either to STDOUT or to STDERR if there is an error). Simple! In addition to the three constants, Ruby also gives you three global variables: $stdin, $stdout, and $stderr. Why would we want these? Well, we probably wouldn't want to reassign a constant to a new I/O method, but if we had a variable, we could point the constants to new methods through the variable. It's easier just to look at an example:

```
record = File.open("/tmp/demo", "w")

$hold_stdout = $stdout
$stdout = record
$stderr = $stdout

puts "We wrote to a file with Ruby!"
divzero = 10/0

record.close
```

The "good stuff" happening here is that first we open a file with write ("w") capabilities. Then, we reassign the current global variable for $stdout to $hold_stdout and assign the current $stdout to the record variable, which is pointing to the file. Just to make sure all of our I/O is covered, we also assign $stderr to $stdout so that any errors are caught and written to our file. We also made sure we had an error by dividing 10 by zero. That ought to do it!

Our output is as expected when we open the file:

```
We wrote to a file with Ruby!
file_demo.rb:8:in '/':
divided by 0 (ZeroDivisionError)
        from file_demo.rb:8:in '<main>'
```

We captured the output we specifically wanted to write, and STDERR helped us out by also writing any errors to the file as well.

With that brief aside into the STDs IN, OUT, and ERR, we can move on to the actual file object itself.

Files

We already saw how to access a file. In the example above, we created and opened for writing a file called demo in a folder called tmp. Let's take a closer look at the options.

A file object represents a physical file somewhere in the system. Thus, you need to define where, exactly, you are planning on creating or finding the file. So creating a file object means pointing it to a file:

```
mode = "r"
file_name = "sample.txt"
f = File.open(file_name, mode)
```

Easy example! The open method will expect to find a file in the current folder named sample.txt. The common "open" modes are:

- "r": read-only
- "w": write-only (overwrites anything in the file, if the file exists)
- "w+": read and write (overwrites anything in the file, if the file exists)
- "a": write-only (append—starts at the end of the file, if the file exists)

Of course, file permissions will play into the access of the files as well, but in most cases you'll be using one of the modes listed. We have already seen writing to files. Reading is just as easy, but a little more background might be helpful before jumping in.

I/O objects are enumerable. That means that the .each method can be used to retrieve one item at a time from the collection. We have already seen this in use with arrays and hashes, but what "items" are in an I/O object? Basically, the items are strings that are terminated with a newline character. If you were to open a standard file and read through it, each "line" would be a string terminated by a newline character. You also saw that in our "console" application. A gets method assumes a newline character as a terminator primarily because you press **Enter** (return) to enter the data. That convention is pretty standard, although there are ways to circumvent it.

The dollar-slash ($/) variable can be used to change what STDIN and STDOUT consider an item. If you used $/ = "DING!" as the end-of-record indicator, you could continue to enter data at the command line until "DING!" was entered, at which time STDIN would consider the record entry done. The most important thing to remember here is that the newline character will be the record terminator unless you define it otherwise. So now it's "I/O, I/O, it's off to work we go."

So now we know that a file object points to an actual file in the system, and that the file will be enumerable so we can iterate through it. What's next? Well, a demo or two might cement this for you.

```ruby
record = File.open("/tmp/demo.txt", "w");
p "Enter your text and press <enter>";
print "Enter 'done' when you are done";
$hold_stdout = $stdout;
$stdout = record;
mytext = "";
while (mytext != "done") do
mytext = gets.chomp
puts mytext
end

record.close;
```

This is very similar to what we looked at before but with a few embellishments. We opened a text file in the tmp folder for writing. We then added a couple of prompts, telling the user to enter text and press **Enter** and to use the word "done" as the indication that they are finished entering data. We then assigned the record (file) to $stdout so that anything we enter is written to the file. We loop until we see "done" as the only thing entered on a line and then close the file. Since we chomp the input and puts the text into the file, we should end up with only a single newline at the end of each line of text. If we didn't chomp (I'm getting hungry!), then we'd have two new lines from gets/puts *and* we'd have to modify the comparison to "done" to be "done\n" because gets would pick up the record each time.

How about reading the file? It's pretty straightforward although there are, again, a couple of things to keep in your mind as you develop code to read the file. Time for another demo.

```
record = File.open("/tmp/demo.txt", "w");
p "Enter your text and press <enter>";
print "Enter 'done' when you are done";
$hold_stdout = $stdout;
$stdout = record;
mytext = "";
while (mytext != "done") do
mytext = gets.chomp
puts mytext
end

record.close;
## Turn off writing to file
$stdout = $hold_stdout
# now open it for reading
record = File.open("/tmp/demo.txt", "r");

puts "Reading the file";

record.each {|l| print l};

record.close;
```

Not a whole lot added. The first thing to attend to is to get our output pointing back to the console, so we take the $stdout object that was on "hold" and reassign the current $stdout to our saved $hold_stdout. If we hadn't done that, then as we read through the file, it would attempt to output to the file, which was opened as read-only anyway but would have caused quite a ruckus. Next, we opened the file as read-only and just added a line to the output to indicate we were now reading through the file. We have a file I/O object, and we know that I/O objects are enumerables, and thus we can use .each, so we do! Using .each passes the enumerated item to the block, which just prints the output. Voilà! We have output!

As an alternative to using the .each method on the file object, you might ask, "Why don't you use read as the method for reading through the file?" Ah! Good question! Read will read the entire file, newlines and all, into memory. Yes, you could do that and print the whole thing in one action, but there aren't many instances where that would make sense. Maybe read a whole file and then write the whole thing out to a screen or page. But in many cases, you'll want something that delivers data in more bite-sized pieces. For that, you can use .each, or you can use the readline method, which will read the data until it gets to the "record separator" character (newline \n in our case). Here is what our code would look like using readline.

```ruby
record = File.open("/tmp/demo.txt", "w");
p "Enter your text and press <enter>";
print "Enter 'done' when you are done";
$hold_stdout = $stdout;
$stdout = record;
mytext = "";
while (mytext != "done") do
mytext = gets.chomp
puts mytext
end

record.close;
## Turn off writing to file
$stdout = $hold_stdout
```

Continued

```
# now open it for reading
record = File.open("/tmp/demo.txt", "r");

puts "Reading the file";

while (!record.eof) do
 mytext = record.readline;

 print mytext
end
record.close;
```

I/O is not the only thing you may want from a file object. Sometimes, you may just want to know if it exists, or is a file or a directory, or is writable. There is a collection of commands that can help here. These don't apply only to files, but also to I/O objects in general.

Does a file exist?

```
FileTest.exist?("/tmp/demo.txt")
```

Is the file a directory? A regular file? A symbolic link?

```
FileTest.directory?("/tmp")
FileTest.file?("/tmp/demo")
FileTest.symlink?("/tmp/demo.txt")
```

Is the file readable? Writable? Executable?

```
FileTest.readable?("/tmp")
FileTest.writable?("/tmp")
FileTest.executable?("/tmp/demo.txt")
```

These methods will return a true/false response. Hopefully, you can see the utility here. Rather than open a file for reading, you may want to use FileTest.exist? and test first, before reading or writing.

System Commands

This section is particularly challenging because we have *two* systems we are dealing with. Ruby really only understands PASE because Ruby is running in PASE (AIX), and that's the world in which it lives. But there is a bigger, more robust universe that the PASE world spins in, and that is IBM i. We dealt with this a bit in the introduction and chapter 2. So let's first deal with the standard, off-the-shelf kind of command that gives us information about PASE. That would be the system command.

On the face of it, you'd think that exec('ls ~') would shell out and return the list of files in your home directory. It *does* return the list, but it exits the current process. So if you are in irb and run exec('ls ~'), then you'll see a list of files, but you'll have exited the irb process. Anything run with exec will do this. Not very handy. A better approach is to use the system command. system("ls ~") will do what you expect: shell out to the system (PASE in our case) and then run the command and return the data. You can also use backticks (` `) around the command as a shortcut, but the results will be a bit different: the values are escaped so that you'll see the '\n' after each entry, rather than a line-by-line list. %x is also shorthand for system and returns results identical to the backtick method. Basically, system will shell out and run the command you requested, returning the data (if there is any) as well as "true" or "false," indicating that it completed without error or not. An example would be something like this:

```
irb(main):009:0> system("which ruby")
/PowerRuby/prV2R1/bin/ruby
=> true

With backticks

`which ruby`

Or %x

%x(which ruby)
```

*NIX geeks love this stuff, so it is no surprise that support for system commands is there, out of the box. But what about IBM i commands? Well, that takes a bit more effort.

The Ruby Toolkit

Here, we have to cross "the great divide" from one OS into another. Right now, depending upon the Matz's Ruby Interpreter (MRI) you are using, you are either living in a non-IBM world or you are in the PASE world. Running the system commands above could be done in Windows, Linux, AIX, Mac, or PASE. The syntax would be similar (though the commands would be executed a bit differently) but pretty much consistent across OSes. That is equally true for access to IBM i commands and programs.

If you read through chapter 4 (and I hope I did a good enough job to leave you with *some* understanding of how XMLSERVICE works), then you already know that we have two entry points into the IBM i world: REST (HTTP) or DB2. The good news is that regardless of what OS you are accessing the IBM i from, the method and approach will be pretty much the same. The best part is that you can build your examples from an OS you feel comfortable with, then move them to PASE pretty much trouble-free.

Although we have both REST and DB2 methods of connecting to IBM i with the toolkit, the preferred method will most often be DB2. If we are dealing with Ruby, which we are, then ActiveRecord will be the means to our ends. There is an ActiveXMLService class that wrappers the ActiveRecord class.

In chapter 4, we talked about the different toolkits and how each of the IBM i open source software (OSS) products already ships with its own. Of course, you can always download the XMLSERVICE library and install and use it as well, but having the toolkit *in* the product makes life simpler. If you are using PowerRuby, you have what you need. If you are using either LUW MRI or JRuby, you can use the XMLSERVICE library or, with JRuby, you could use the JTOpen tools (are those enough options for you?).

Let's start simply, by looking at a standalone Ruby script using ActiveRecord to connect to IBM i and run a command. Here is the code:

```
require 'xmlservice'
require 'yaml'
```
Continued

```
data=YAML::load(File.read("credentials.yml"));

user = data["user"]
password = data["password"]

ActiveXMLService::Base.establish_connection(
   connection: 'ActiveRecord', adapter: 'ibm_db', database: '*LOCAL',
   username: "#{user}", password: "#{password}"
)

wrksysval = XMLService::I_SH.new("system -i 'WRKSYSVAL SYSVAL(QTIME)
OUTPUT(*PRINT)'")
wrksysval.xmlservice
puts wrksysval.out_xml
```

You know this stuff, but let's walk though it anyway. The first require brings in the resources for XMLSERVICE. There is an xmlservice gem file that is a wrapper for the XMLSERVICE library that ultimately is called. The second require brings in resources to read the YAML file. YAML (Yet Another Markup Language) is used quite a bit for setting configuration options for Ruby apps. In this case, I used a YAML file to store the credentials, so we don't have hard-coded credentials in our code, and if we need to, we can change the credentials in the file for *all* the scripts that might use it. Immediately below the YAML require is the reference to the YAML file itself being loaded into a variable called data. Then we assign the values from the data object into variables for user ID and password, which we in turn use to connect to IBM i.

Next comes the real meat of the script, calling the command on IBM i. We do that in a bit of a sneaky way by invoking a shell script in PASE.

```
wrksysval = XMLService::I_SH.new("system -i 'WRKSYSVAL SYSVAL(QTIME)
OUTPUT(*PRINT)'")
```

The call to I_SH.new ("I" being IBM i and "SH" being a shell invocation) builds a PASE system call, which, in turn, calls a "native" IBM command and outputs to a PRINT job, which is piped back to the XMLSERVICE call and is returned to the WRKSYSVAL object. The wrkactjob.xmlservice is the call to run the script. The puts statement outputs the text, which is basically the printed output from the call. Pretty straightforward.

We can also take the REST approach and use the REST interface to make the call. That script looks slightly different:

```ruby
require 'xmlservice'
require 'yaml'

data=YAML::load(File.read("credentials.yml"));

user = data["user"]
password = data["password"]

ActiveXMLService::Base.establish_connection(
  connection: "http://10.0.10.205:7070/cgi-bin/xmlcgi.pgm",
  username: "#{user}",
    password: "#{password}"
)

wrksysval = XMLService::I_SH.new("system -i 'WRKSYSVAL SYSVAL(QTIME)
OUTPUT(*PRINT)'")
wrksysval.xmlservice
puts wrksysval.out_xml  #nice
```

In this slightly different script, our ActiveXMLService class method that makes the connection uses a REST (HTTP) connection type rather than an ActiveRecord type of connection. Unknown to you, but known to me because of the IP address listed, is the fact that the REST call is being made to a different partition (it could have been across the world). So REST can be a handy way to grab data from a remote system.

The result is the same: a text file containing the *PRINT output from the WRKSYSVAL (Work with System Value) command is returned and displayed in the puts statement.

```
<?xml version='1.0'?>
<myscript>
<sh error='fast'>
<![CDATA[                      System Values          Page    1
5770SS1 V7R1M0   100423          VAS2         09/18/16  09:21:14 MDT
                 Current              Shipped
 Name            value               value         Description
 QTIME           09:21:14            '    '         Time of day
 Note:   > means current value is different from the shipped value
              * * * * *   E N D   O F   L I S T I N G   * * * * *]]>
</sh>
</myscript>
```

No surprises! Calling a program takes a little more work, just like it does when you invoke XMLSERVICE from a POST. With program calls, you have parameters to pass and data, perhaps, to return, so there is more involved. Let's begin by looking at the incredibly complex program we are going to call. RPG, of course:

```
dcl-pr demo1 extpgm;
    char1 char(1);
    dec1 packed(7:4);
end-pr;
dcl-pi demo1;
   char1 char(1);
   dec1 packed(7:4);
end-pi;

 char1 = 'C';
 dec1 = 321.1234;
 return;
```

Doncha just *love* free-format RPG? We have a simple RPG program with a single procedure that basically sets two variables and returns. How would we call that program? Well, here's how:

```
require 'xmlservice'
require 'yaml'

data=YAML::load(File.read("credentials.yml"));

user = data["user"]
password = data["password"]

ActiveXMLService::Base.establish_connection(
    connection: 'ActiveRecord', adapter: 'ibm_db', database: '*LOCAL',
    username: "#{user}", password: "#{password}"
)

pgm = XMLService::I_PGM.new('DEMO1', 'RUBYDEMO') <<
 XMLService::I_a.new('inchara',1,'Z') <<
 XMLService::I_p.new('indec1',7,4,11.1111)

pgm.xmlservice

puts pgm.to_xml

puts "input parm0: #{pgm.input.PARM0.inchara}"
puts "input parm1: #{pgm.input.PARM1.indec1}"
puts "------------------------------------------"
puts "output parm0: #{pgm.response.PARM0.inchara}"
puts "output parm1: #{pgm.response.PARM1.indec1}"
```

The first 14 or so lines are familiar. They just set up the connection stuff. Starting with the pgm variable, things get more interesting. Now we have an I_PGM.new method to create a call to an RPG program (as opposed to the I_SH.new method that set up the shell script call). In our XMLService call, we define two parameters: an I_a type and an I_p type, both of which are defined as "io" parms so they can be used for both input and output. We RPGers know what data types "a" and "p" mean ("alphabetic" and "packed"), so we know we are passing a character and a number. We pass in a Z and the number 11.1111.

Looking at the program, we know that what will be returned is a "C" and a 321.1234—at least, we *hope* that is what we get back. Let's call it!

```
<pgm name='DEMO1' lib='RUBYDEMO' error='fast'>
<parm var='PARM0' io='io'>
<data var='inchara' type='1a'>Z</data>
</parm>
<parm var='PARM1' io='io'>
<data var='indec1' type='7p4'>11.1111</data>
</parm>
</pgm>
input parm0: Z
input parm1: 11.1111
-------------------------------------------
output parm0: C
output parm1: 321.1234
```

Nice! The object returned by the XMLService call contains the in and out parameters, as you can see from the puts statements: puts "input parm0: #{pgm.input.PARM0.inchara}". Here, pgm contains an input object that contains a PARM0 object named 'inchara', which contains the value of the parameter.

Your challenge in calling an RPG program will probably be in defining the parameters and types. There is a listing here: *http://yips.idevcloud.com/wiki/index.php/XMLService/ DataTypes*. But as I said before, these URLs can move, so check my website (*petesworkshop.com*) or *common.org* or, well, you know how to use Google. Try that!

Alternatives

We still have a couple of other ways to skin this cat. You can, and will with Rails, use the ActiveRecord gem to directly I/O to a DB2 database. You'll probably head this direction with Rails, but you might have some need to read and/or write directly to DB2 on IBM i without the overhead of Rails. Let's take a look at an example that would run an SQL statement directly and return the data.

This example is a bit long, but it will show you the process of creating a table, populating it with data, and then reading though that data. Some of it should be familiar territory.

```ruby
#!/usr/bin/env ruby
require 'active_record'
require 'yaml'

data=YAML::load(File.read("credentials.yml"));

user = data["user"]
password = data["password"]

ActiveRecord::Base.establish_connection(
  :adapter => 'ibm_db',
  :username=> "#{user}",
  :password =>  "#{password}",
  :database => '*LOCAL',
  :schema => 'empDemo'
  )

# Create a table in the schema

ActiveRecord::Schema.define do

    create_table :employees do |table|
     table.column :emp_id, :integer
        table.column :firstname, :string, limit: 30
        table.column :lastname, :string, limit: 50
        table.column :address, :string, limit: 60
        table.column :city, :string, limit: 40
        table.column :st, :string, limit: 10
        table.column :zip, :string, limit: 9
    end
end

class Employee < ActiveRecord::Base
```

Continued

```
end

emp = Employee.create(:emp_id => 22,:firstname => 'Chester', :lastname=>
'BesterTester',:address=>'123 East Main Street',:city=>'San Antonio',:st
=>'Texas',:zip=>'78258')
emp = Employee.create(:emp_id => 44,:firstname => 'Mister', :lastname=>'
Master',:address=>'222 East Oak Street',:city=>'San Antonio',:st=>'Texas
',:zip=>'78255')
emp = Employee.create(:emp_id => 62,:firstname => 'Peekup', :lastname=>'
Andropov',:address=>'321 West Street',:city=>'San Antonio',:st=>'Texas',
:zip=>'78253')

## Alternate method
emp = Employee.new

emp.emp_id = 64
emp.firstname = 'Peekup'
emp.lastname='AndPeekupAgain'
emp.address = '999 Baltimore Street'
emp.city='San Antonio'
emp.st='Texas'
emp.zip='78251'

emp.save


puts '-------------------------------'
puts Employee.find_by_id(1).lastname
puts Employee.find_by_emp_id(62).lastname
puts Employee.find_by_firstname('Peekup').lastname
puts Employee.find_by_lastname('Master').firstname
puts '-------------------------------'
Employee.find_each do |empl|
puts empl.firstname << ' ' << empl.lastname
end
```

Continued

```
puts '-----------------------------'
Employee.where("firstname = 'Peekup'").find_each do |empl|
puts empl.firstname << ' ' << empl.lastname
end
puts '-----------------------------'
#ActiveRecord::Migration.drop_table(:employees)
```

The first 17 lines should be familiar. We require 'active_record' and 'yaml' gems and set up the connection. The only things that are different in the connection are that we are using ActiveRecord instead of ActiveXML or REST, and also we reference a schema (library) where the table will be stored (empDemo).

With the connection established, we then create a new definition in the schema, which turns out to be a "table" definition where a table called employees is defined:

```
ActiveRecord::Schema.define do

    create_table :employees do |table|
        table.column :emp_id, :integer
        table.column :firstname, :string, limit: 30
        table.column :lastname, :string, limit: 50
        table.column :address, :string, limit: 60
        table.column :city, :string, limit: 40
        table.column :st, :string, limit: 10
        table.column :zip, :string, limit: 9
    end
end
```

So far so good. Next, we subclass the ActiveRecord::Base class, so we inherit the ActiveRecord Base class methods:

```
class Employee < ActiveRecord::Base

end
```

Next, we create new records by using the Base class create method:

```
emp = Employee.create(:emp_id => 22,:firstname => 'Chester', :lastname=>
'BesterTester',:address=>'123 East Main Street',:city=>'San Antonio',:st
=>'Texas',:zip=>'78258')
```

Lather, rinse, and repeat.

We can also create new database records by first instantiating a new object, populating the properties, and then saving it to the database. To wit:

```
## Alternate method
emp = Employee.new

emp.emp_id = 64
emp.firstname = 'Peekup'
emp.lastname='AndPeekupAgain'
emp.address = '999 Baltimore Street'
emp.city='San Antonio'
emp.st='Texas'
emp.zip='78251'


emp.save
```

Finally, here are a couple of ways to retrieve and display the records:

```
puts '--------------------------------'
puts Employee.find_by_id(1).lastname
puts Employee.find_by_emp_id(62).lastname
puts Employee.find_by_firstname('Peekup').lastname
puts Employee.find_by_lastname('Master').firstname
puts '--------------------------------'
Employee.find_each do |emp|
                                                        Continued
```

```
puts empl.firstname << ' ' << empl.lastname
end
puts '-------------------------------'
Employee.where("firstname = 'Peekup'").find_each do |empl|
puts empl.firstname << ' ' << empl.lastname
end
puts '-------------------------------'
#ActiveRecord::Migration.drop_table(:employees)
```

The code below the first puts '----' line outputs a property of a record found by using the find method. The "finds" are generated based on the columns created in the table. So, without having to create the methods, you immediately have a find_by method for each column. The puts simply outputs a property of the "found" record.

The code below the second puts '----' line simply iterates through the records returned by find_each, which returns a collection of Employee records. In this particular example, we just output the firstname and lastname properties.

The code below the third puts '----' line simply iterates through the records returned by a where clause followed by a find_each, which returns a collection of Employee records with a firstname property of 'Peekup'. In this example, we again just output the firstname and lastname properties even though all columns of data are available in the object returned.

Using JRuby with ActiveXMLService and ActiveRecord

We haven't touched on how to approach accessing IBM i resources from Ruby if we choose to use the JRuby MRI. JRuby offers another option that we can explore, which is connecting through JDBC using the JTOpen driver. JTOpen opens a whole other world to JRuby because JTOpen has many API entry points to allow us to access IBM i resources. I created a class that implemented a few of these APIs, so let's take a look.

The first part of the file contains a "preamble" that explains how the class works and how to load it (mostly to assist my failing memory).

```
class JtoI

## to use this class, you will need to be in the same folder as
## jt400.jar or have it on your classpath
## Load the file: load "drive_and_pathname/JtoI.rb"
## Create an instance of it:   rdemo = JtoI.new()
## establish a connection:   rdemo.connect('IP','USER','PASSWORD')
## run the listspoolfiles method:  rdemo.listspoolfiles('LIB','OUTQ')
## that's it

## Class variables
@@system = nil
@@sysIP=nil
@@user=nil
@@pass=nil

## the necessary requires - Java and the Jtopen (jt400) jar
require 'java'
require 'jt400.jar'

## This is a little different from the usual Ruby directives.
## This actually tells JRuby which Java classes to load based
## on package names
include_package 'com.ibm.as400.access'
include_package 'com.ibm.as400.access.AS400Message'
include_package 'com.ibm.as400.access.CommandCall'

## This pulls in classes from the Java language that will be used
## by JRuby
## In this particular case, I am using these system classes to load
## the properties file.
## Could I do this in Ruby? Yes! They are here as examples
java_import 'java.util.Properties'
java_import 'java.io.FileInputStream'
java_import 'java.io.InputStreamReader'
java_import 'java.lang.StringBuffer'
```

With the setup out of the way, we can take a look at implementation.

```
## this loads the properties file:

def get_properties_from_file
  props = Properties.new
  fileInput = FileInputStream.new("ibmi.properties")
  props.load(fileInput)
  fileInput.close
  props
end

## This simply lets us know that we have successfully initialized
## the class

def initialize

puts "Ready"

end

## We need to connect to the IBM i, so we have what we need in
## the properties file
## Yeah, we could also use a YAML file
def connect()

  props = get_properties_from_file

  @@sysIP=props['ip']
  @@user=props['user']
  @@pass=props['password']

  @@system = AS400.new(@@sysIP,@@user,@@pass)

  if @@system != nil
    puts 'Connected'
  end

end
```

Once we call the connect method on the instance, we can do something useful. In this case, we will list some spool files.

```ruby
def listspoolfiles(lib, outq)

  puts "Now receiving all spooled files synchronously"

  splfList = SpooledFileList.new(@@system )
  splfList.setUserFilter("*ALL")
  splfList.setQueueFilter("/QSYS.LIB/"+lib+".LIB/"+outq+".OUTQ")

  # open list, openSynchronously() returns when the list is completed.
  splfList.openSynchronously()

  ## Get a map containing the spool file objects
  splobjs = splfList.getObjects()

  ## Interate through the objects
  splobjs.map do |splf|
  splfName = splf.getName() # SpooledFile.ATTR_SPOOLFILE = 104
  splfNum = splf.getNumber()
  jobName = splf.getStringAttribute(PrintObject::ATTR_JOBNAME)
  jobUser = splf.getStringAttribute(PrintObject::ATTR_SPLF_CREATOR)
  jobNum = splf.getJobNumber()

  ## Output some info
  puts splfName  <<" " << jobName <<" "<< jobUser <<" "<< jobNum

  ## Output the text of the spooled file
  getSpoolFile(splf)

end

# clean up after we are done with the list
splfList.close

end
```

Continued

```ruby
def getSpoolFile(splf)

#
p1 =  PrintParameterList.new()
p1.setParameter(SpooledFile::ATTR_MFGTYPE, "*WSCST")
p1.setParameter(SpooledFile::ATTR_WORKSTATION_CUST_OBJECT, "/QSYS.LIB/
QWPDEFAULT.WSCST")
inpStream = splf.getTransformedInputStream(p1)
isr = java.io.InputStreamReader.new(inpStream)
# Read the input stream buffer and create a string buffer
buf = Java::char[32767].new
        buffer = java.lang.StringBuffer.new
        if isr.ready
            bytesRead = 0
            bytesRead = isr.read(buf, 0, buf.length)
            while ( bytesRead != -1 )
                #puts bytesRead
                if bytesRead > 0
                    #buffer.append(java.lang.String.new
                    (buf,0,bytesRead) )
                    puts java.lang.String.new(buf,0,bytesRead)
                end
                bytesRead = isr.read(buf, 0, buf.length)
            end
        end

end
```

An example of a script that uses this class would be:

```ruby
#IBM i jruby demo
## Change this path to your OWN
load "/home/pete/demos/jruby/JtoI.rb"
```
                                                                Continued

```
rdemo = JtoI.new()
rdemo.conn()
rdemo.listspoolfiles('QGPL','QPRINT2')
```

The thing that blows the minds of some folks who work with Java and Ruby in this environment is the interspersing of both the Ruby and Java code. For someone who works in Java most of the time, it is sometimes easier just to call the Java APIs that you need rather than use Ruby. In some cases, where there isn't an equivalent, you just call the Java classes directly.

What I like about this approach is that you don't have to have all the Java stuff (JTOpen, in this case) wrappered in Ruby methods. You can use what you want. I can see an advantage, though, to wrappering the JTOpen APIs so that it is possible to call all the IBM i commands and APIs from Ruby. At some point, I'd love to create a new project that either does wrapper this stuff or allows me to just tweak the Ruby toolkit to use JDBC for connecting. With a little time, maybe I will.

There is a simpler example to look at, and that would be creating an interactive SQL command process (a very basic one). It looks like this:

```
def runSQLCmd

va = ["jdbc:as400://#{@@sysIP}","#{@@user}","#{@@pass}"]

com.ibm.as400.access.jdbcClient.Main.main va

end
```

Ridiculously simple. Especially when you invoke it with a snippet of script:

```
#IBM i SQL demo
## Change this line to your OWN path in the IFS
load "/home/pete/demos/jruby/JtoI.rb"
```
Continued

```
rdemo = JtoI.new()
rdemo.connect()
puts 'Run an SQL command:'
rdemo.runSQLCmd()
```

You'll be prompted for an SQL command. I just ran this simple Select:

```
Ready
Connected
Run an SQL command:
>select * from employee.employee
EMPID,EMPFNAME,EMPLNAME,EMPADDRESS,EMPCITY,EMPSTATE,EMPZIP,
EMPEMAIL,PASS_WORD
1,Admin,Administrator,12345 Mainly Street,Anytown2,UT,84111,
cbestertester@gmail.com,PASSWORD
2,Charlie,BesterTester,1234 Ash,Anytown,UT,84999,
tester@gmail.com,PASSWORD
3,Seeme,Going,12 East Oak,Anytown,UT,84117,yettanutha@gmail.com,PASSWORD
4,Nuthin,Doing,156 Main,MyTwon,TN,43221,bubba@gmail.com,PASSWORD
5,Peekop,Andropoff,444 East St,MyTown,TN,0000,demo@gmail.com,PASSWORD
6,Andy,Rooney,111 Sin Street,Reno,NV,77711,petereno@reno.com,PASSWORD
7,Maybe,Later,123 East Main,SLC,UT,99999,
something@something.com,PASSWORD
```

It isn't pretty, but it's serviceable. Note that the script instantiates the class (rdemo = JtoI.new()), and the initialization routine responds with "Ready." Then we connect with rdemo.connect(), and the method responds with "Connected." Then our puts statement prompts us for the command, which I entered as select * from employee.employee. Bingo! We got our output! Simple. Powerful.

You could also build a simple command processor:

```
def runCommand(cmdText)

cmd = CommandCall.new(@@system)

cmd.run("#{cmdText}")

## Print out the messages that came back
messageList = cmd.getMessageList() # ArrayList?

messageList.each { |msg|  puts "Message "<<  msg.getText }

end
```

Nothing fancy, but it gets the job done.

This is *exactly* why I love open source on IBM i! There are so many different yet very powerful ways to get the job done.

Something New

The whole purpose of this chapter was to whet your appetite for trying something new and innovative. Try to solve a difficult problem as cleverly as you can. These tools are fun to use and have wonderful capabilities. Go for it!

7

Rails and Ruby

Originally I was going to include the Rails chapter in the Ruby chapter, because, well, most folks who are interested in Ruby are going to use Rails for creating Web applications. You don't *have* to use Rails for Web development in the Ruby language; there are other Web frameworks out there that are written in Ruby: Sinatra, Padrino (based on Sinatra), Cuba (aiy!), Cramp, Hanami, and a bunch of others. But Rails is the 800-pound gorilla, so we are going to check it out. I didn't include it in the Ruby chapter because, well, remember what happened to the alien heads in the movie *Mars Attacks!* when the yodeling started ... OK, you get the picture. You may need a minute or two to decompress from all the new stuff thrown at you in the Ruby chapter. We'll take a look at the structure and components of a Rails app, and we'll get you started in the Rails-building business, but that is about it. The Ruby chapter introduced you to the "getting to IBM i" parts, and there is certainly much on the Internet on how to create Rails applications. The good news here is that PowerRuby makes building Rails apps on IBM i drop-dead simple. With that foundation, you can build with confidence!

Getting Started with Rails

Rails has been around since 2005, which makes it a "mature" product. In fact, it has been around *so* long that you'll need to be careful about which version of Ruby you are running and what version of Rails is supported on that version of Ruby. Most of the time, you won't have to give it a second thought because the version of Rails that you download and the version of Ruby that you download will usually be compatible. But in the case of IBM i–specific implementations, you might find yourself running a slightly older version of Ruby and thus might need to be aware of that version when installing other gems that may be needed. The good news with an IBM i–specific implementation like PowerRuby is that the gems you will need should already be installed for Rails, so you won't have to go through the convoluted steps to get the gem versions aligned with Ruby and Rails.

So what is a *gem*? Well, in keeping with the "jewelry" motif of the Ruby name, a gem is a package manager that can install components of a Ruby program. Gems encapsulate functionality into a downloadable module that can be installed automatically. There are tens of thousands, maybe hundreds of thousands, of gems at *https://rubygems.org*. They have been contributed by the Ruby community and cover a wide variety of needs and functions. Rails itself is a gem (a big one), and Rails has, at last count ... well, it's really hard to count because some gems have dependencies on other gems that may depend on other gems and ... you get the picture. The best part about gems is that they are pretty much self-managing, so you won't have to install things individually or check dependencies. If your IBM i has access to an Internet connection, the gem install command will pretty much handle everything.

The basics of a Rails installation are pretty easy, then. After you have successfully installed Ruby (PowerRuby or JRuby on IBM i), you just run gem install rails if you are running Ruby on Windows or Linux, or JRuby on IBM i. If you are running PowerRuby on IBM i, you don't have to do anything. Rails comes "bundled" with PowerRuby, so you'll already have a compatible version after you finish installing PowerRuby. And, speaking of "bundled," in most cases, when you do run a gem install ..., you'll see Bundler running last as "bundle install." Bundler really does all the heavy lifting. You'll find more information about Bundler at *http://bundler.io/*.

If you were to create a new gem that had dependencies on other gems, you would create a Gemfile in your gem. Then, once your gem was installed, you'd run a bundle install command, and the Gemfile would tell Bundler what other gems to install so your gem will work. The Gemfile specifies minimum (and sometimes maximum) gem versions that your gem needs. But, it's pretty cool, all in all. I find the process of installing Rails very similar to downloading and installing PTFs on IBM i, although Bundler is much more automated. Bundler pretty much ensures that all the correct components are in place after going through the process of installing a gem. Anyone who has slid down into "dependency hell" with a Linux installation (or AIX/PASE, for that matter) will appreciate the simplicity that Bundler brings to the Ruby/Rails table.

Building a Rails Application

Once Rails is installed, you begin to build your Rails app through a series of commands that create specific components of the Rails app. You start with the command rails new and give the application a name that becomes the base folder of the application. The classic Rails tutorial will walk you through building a blogging application—so you might see a command like this:

```
rails new myblog
```

A boatload of folders and files will follow:

```
E:\RailsApps>rails new myblog
    create
    create    README.rdoc
    create    Rakefile
    create    config.ru
    create    .gitignore
    create    Gemfile
    create    app
    create    app/assets/javascripts/application.js
    create    app/assets/stylesheets/application.css
    create    app/controllers/application_controller.rb
    create    app/helpers/application_helper.rb
    create    app/views/layouts/application.html.erb
    create    app/assets/images/.keep
    create    app/mailers/.keep
    create    app/models/.keep
    create    app/controllers/concerns/.keep
    create    app/models/concerns/.keep
    create    bin
    create    bin/bundle
```

```
create  bin/rails
create  bin/rake
create  bin/setup
create  config
create  config/routes.rb
create  config/application.rb
create  config/environment.rb
create  config/secrets.yml
create  config/environments
create  config/environments/development.rb
create  config/environments/production.rb
create  config/environments/test.rb
create  config/initializers
create  config/initializers/assets.rb
create  config/initializers/backtrace_silencers.rb
create  config/initializers/cookies_serializer.rb
create  config/initializers/filter_parameter_logging
create  config/initializers/inflections.rb
create  config/initializers/mime_types.rb
create  config/initializers/session_store.rb
create  config/initializers/wrap_parameters.rb
create  config/locales
create  config/locales/en.yml
create  config/boot.rb
create  config/database.yml
create  db
create  db/seeds.rb
create  lib
create  lib/tasks
create  lib/tasks/.keep
create  lib/assets
create  lib/assets/.keep
create  log
create  log/.keep
create  public
create  public/404.html
create  public/422.html
```

```
create   public/500.html
create   public/favicon.ico
create   public/robots.txt
create   test/fixtures
create   test/fixtures/.keep
create   test/controllers
create   test/controllers/.keep
create   test/mailers
create   test/mailers/.keep
create   test/models
create   test/models/.keep
create   test/helpers
create   test/helpers/.keep
create   test/integration
create   test/integration/.keep
create   test/test_helper.rb
create   tmp/cache
create   tmp/cache/assets
create   vendor/assets/javascripts
create   vendor/assets/javascripts/.keep
create   vendor/assets/stylesheets
create   vendor/assets/stylesheets/.keep
   run   bundle install
Fetching gem metadata from https://rubygems.org/
Fetching version metadata from https://rubygems.org/
Fetching dependency metadata from https://rubygems.org/
Resolving dependencies....................................
```

So you can see that the final command was bundle install, and then there was a LOOONNGG pause (at least for me), and then the output:

```
Using rake 11.2.2
Using i18n 0.7.0
Using json 1.8.3
Using minitest 5.9.0
Using thread_safe 0.3.5
Using builder 3.2.2
```

```
Using erubis 2.7.0
Using nokogiri 1.6.8
Using rack 1.6.4
Using mime-types 2.99.2
Using arel 6.0.3
Using jdbc-sqlite3 3.8.11.2
Using bundler 1.12.5
Using coffee-script-source 1.10.0
Using execjs 2.7.0
Using thor 0.19.1
Using concurrent-ruby 1.0.2
Using multi_json 1.12.1
Using sass 3.4.22
Using tilt 2.0.5
Using therubyrhino_jar 1.7.6
Using turbolinks-source 5.0.0
Using rdoc 4.2.2
Using tzinfo 1.2.2
Using loofah 2.0.3
Using rack-test 0.6.3
Using mail 2.6.4
Installing coffee-script 2.4.1
Installing uglifier 3.0.0
Using sprockets 3.7.0
Installing therubyrhino 2.0.4
Installing turbolinks 5.0.0
Installing sdoc 0.4.1
Using activesupport 4.2.5
Installing tzinfo-data 1.2016.6
Using rails-html-sanitizer 1.0.3
Using rails-deprecated_sanitizer 1.0.3
Using globalid 0.3.6
Using activemodel 4.2.5
Installing jbuilder 2.6.0
Using rails-dom-testing 1.0.7
Using activejob 4.2.5
Using activerecord 4.2.5
```

```
Using actionview 4.2.5
Installing activerecord-jdbc-adapter 1.3.20
Using actionpack 4.2.5
Installing activerecord-jdbcsqlite3-adapter 1.3.20
Using actionmailer 4.2.5
Using railties 4.2.5
Using sprockets-rails 3.1.1
Installing coffee-rails 4.1.1
Installing jquery-rails 4.1.1
Using rails 4.2.5
Installing sass-rails 5.0.6
Bundle complete! 11 Gemfile dependencies, 54 gems now installed.
Use 'bundle show [gemname]' to see where a bundled gem is installed.
```

The using/installing pattern will be long or short, depending upon how many gems were already installed at the proper level. In this case, 11 new gems were installed. Again, the PowerRuby installation installs most of the required Gems initially for you.

At this point, reviewing the long listing on the last few pages, you might come to the conclusion that Rails is pretty structured. In fact, it is highly opinionated (like that long-winded brother-in-law). The oft-quoted "We can do this the hard way or the easy way" phrase comes to mind. Rails stresses convention over configuration, so if you play by the Rails rules, things will go easy for you. If not, you'll be spending a "night in the box" (for you *Cool Hand Luke* fans). So let's explore those rules a bit. If you really want a full-blown Rails experience, there are many tutorials out there, not the least of which are those at *https://guides.rubyonrails.org* or *https://www.railstutorial.org/*. The goal here is to ground you in the basics of Rails development and, in the process, maybe give you some ideas of how you could structure your code even if you are not running Rails.

Rails and MVC

The first thing to tackle is the basic, overall structure of the framework. Rails is a Model-View-Controller, or MVC framework. You may have heard the term "MVC" before, but like most TLAs (three-letter acronyms), you probably just nodded your head with a glazed look in your eyes and said, "yeah, got it."

The part of MVC that is easiest to understand is the *view* part, which in the Web world is probably some kind of HTML output. Most often, the HTML file that is output isn't completely created on the fly: a template is used to format the page with "placeholders" that indicate where dynamic data will go. Templates in the Rails world, by convention, are .erb files (.erb stands for *embedded Ruby file*). In many ways, an .erb file is like the DDS for a display file. You lay out where text and dynamic content reside, and, going one better than a display file, indicate where pictures, other images, links, and other content go. Unlike a "pure" HTML page, the .erb file can contain Ruby scripting directives as well, so then it begins to look like a PHP, JSP, or .aspx page. Rails also takes advantage of *partials*, which are segments of a page that can be included when an entire page is rendered. So a common segment of HTML can be encapsulated in a partial, and that partial can then be included, rather than recreating or copying the same segment over and over again.

With the easy part of MVC out of the way, the last two parts, *model* and *controller*, have to be dealt with, and we already muddied the waters for view. Stepping back for a moment, remember how I said that an .erb file can contain some Ruby scripting? Well, that breaks the purist version of view. View should be view, period, but these days it is rare to have a pure view; often the view will contain scripting that moves or manipulates data independently of the model or controller. The model is typically where data for the application is managed. You could call it the "business logic" of the application. It operates on data, applies rules, and responds to requests. The controller handles the "operational logic." This could be something like handling data input and output, or it may be dispatching requests to the model or interacting with a service. But as much as MVC is supposed to represent a "separation of concerns" (a good thing), in most cases it is about as easy to separate each concern as separating conjoined triplets. Nevertheless, it is good practice to keep the M and the V and the C separate in your head as you write code. Doing so can help you build more modular, maintainable code, and if you do it right, you can DRY out your code so each piece is reusable in your app. (DRY stands for Don't Repeat Yourself, a familiar precept in the Ruby world.)

The reason I bring up the MVC pattern is that you'll see it in Rails, in spades. When you ran the rails new myblog command or the RAILSNEW command in PowerRuby and built that initial framework, it structured the components in an MVC way. So, thinking in terms of MVC structure, MVC will also help you find stuff (usually) in your Rails project.

Structure of a Rails Project

Figure 7.1 shows the beast you create with rails new:

```
▼  ☐ myblog  E:\Workspaces\rails\myblog
    ▶  ☐ app
    ▶  ☐ bin
    ▶  ☐ config
    ▶  ☐ db
    ▶  ☐ lib
    ▶  ☐ log
    ▶  ☐ public
    ▶  ☐ test
    ▶  ☐ tmp
    ▶  ☐ vendor
       ☐ .gitignore
       ☐ config.ru
       ☐ Gemfile
       ☐ Gemfile.lock
       ☐ Rakefile
       ☐ README.rdoc
```

Figure 7.1: Sample Rails project components

The app folder is where most of the code for your app lives. We'll circle back to it in a second. The bin folder is where the gem wrappers (*binstubs*) live. These were introduced in Rails version 4 and provide a way for multiple Rails and Ruby environments to coexist. The config folder is where the configuration scripts and properties live, so that you can configure database connections, routes for your application, and a bunch of other options. The db folder is where your database schemas will live along with *migrations*, a cool feature of Rails that we'll explore momentarily. The lib folder will contain extended modules for your application. The log folder will contain (right you are!) logs generated by your application. The public folder will contain static content that your base app will serve. The test folder will contain your unit tests if you decide to create them. The tmp folder will contain temporary files that your application might generate, such as cache files and PID references.

We already covered the Gemfile, but the Rakefile is something worth noting here. Rake is a task-oriented script file that will execute a series of rake commands. Rake is similar to the makefile in C in that you can set configuration options and run steps in sequence to build or modify your application. It is basically a task-automation tool.

So, back to the app folder. This folder contains subfolders for the application structure. You should immediately see the model, view, and controller folders and get a sense of what they do. model will be empty for now because we really don't have an app designed, so no logic for it has been written. view has a layout folder in it, and that is where your .erb templates will live that apply to the entire app. This structure can get quite complex over time as partials are added for other controllers that might be created. But, generally, your templates live here. The controller folder will house the classes that control input from your users and access to your Web pages.

There are a couple of other folders in the app folder that fall outside the MVC convention. The assets folder has images, JavaScript, and CSS content that is served by your app. The helpers folder contains small sections of code that usually render a component of a page (view) so you aren't cluttering up your controller folder. The mailers folder will contain code for your email functions should your application need them. Rails' Action Mailer is your friend here.

Database Access in Rails

Database access in Rails is one of the cool features that you'll soon wish was present in every application on all the platforms and frameworks you work with. To my knowledge, Rails is the only place where this feature is so nicely implemented. Before you start thinking that *all* applications have database access, so what is so "cool" about Rails, let me tell you how it works. It starts with a "generate" statement. Rails uses the generate command to create different components, so that you don't have to hand tool each component and thus possibly introduce something that unintentionally breaks the "convention" rule. We are going to start with the model in our Rails app, so we use this command to create a model for our blog:

```
rails generate model Article title:string text:text
```

We are starting out *very* slowly, but there is quite a bit of magic in that one statement. The response to the command is that Rails spews out quite a few files. We have articles.rb suddenly appearing in app/models and we have something called migrate/20160728231232_create_articles.rb in the db folder. "*What* is that?" you ask. That, my friend, is *magic*! What Rails did was create a script to create a database table. The reason for the funky name and the reason it lurks in the migrate folder is because it will track every change to the database we make *and* allow us to roll back stuff if we need to. The "going forward" is probably a logical step for you to think about. Yeah, it *would* be nice to know what each change was to the schema in a database. But, going back, that seems pretty weird.

There is another rabbit hole we *could* go down but won't, but the reason that tracking forward changes and rolling them back in development is so important is because of agile development techniques. Like I said, we are *not* going down that rabbit hole—but basically agile focuses on rapid prototyping, iterative development, evolving design, and rapid coding. Essentially it means the app can change drastically through the development lifecycle by working closely with the target customer, constantly checking to see if you were on the right track versus taking the spec (which is usually terrible) and writing the code and *then* showing it to the customer, who will probably say: "No, that isn't what I wanted." So, if you are in an agile world, your code, and therefore your database, will change. Being able to roll back database changes quickly and easily is a real plus.

When you run the migration, the table will be created. With each subsequent change to the model, a migration will be created, which will modify the model and the table structure and migrate the data to the new table structure. Pretty cool, huh?

Accessing Resources with Routes

Rails is also a RESTful framework, so you will see references to things called *routes*. Very simply, routes are a way for the framework to evaluate a request for a resource and map it to a function or a page. In RPG 5250 programming, you point directly to the resources and program your overall application will use, either by invoking them directly with a "call pgmB" kind of syntax or indirectly through a menu that performs those calls for you. In the Web world, the Uniform Resource Identifier (URI) is the pointer to a resource somewhere in the vast expanse that is the Internet. A typical URI might be something like this:

```
https://developer.mozilla.org/en-US/docs/Web/JavaScript/Reference/
Classes
```

This is a RESTful URI. The actual resource type isn't known or referenced. It could be a PDF, an HTML page, or an MP4 video. You can't tell even whether the HTTP method used is a GET, PUT, POST, or DELETE. But your application will know by reading the request and the route, which will be some part or parts of the URI that are separated by the slash (/). Rails evaluates the route automatically and will search for the correct route in your config/routes.rb script that you defined and point it to your controller.

For example, let's say that your nifty blog application resides at 10.0.10.205. Your user, either directly or through a link, requests http://10.0.10.205/articles/42. In your config/routes.rb script, you might have something like this:

```
Rails.application.routes.draw do
    get 'articles/:id'

    root 'articles#show'
end
```

Of course this also assumes that you have created the controller for articles and have a show method defined. But this means that your http://10.0.10.205/articles/42 renders to, perhaps, an HTML page. Or, if you wanted to change the output, you could maybe have it return a PDF and make that change with very little effort.

Summing It Up

The remainder of coding your Rails app is really outside the scope of this book. There are plenty of very good tutorials on building a Rails app, which will get even the most de-Railed person up to speed quickly. But, here are the takeaways:

1. Rails development can be rapid because it follows the "convention over configuration" mantra. You play by the rules, you get an app, fast!
2. Rails accommodates agile development techniques that allow you to rapidly change your app during and after development.
3. Rails is RESTful, which can contribute to more modular and readable code.

Take some time to a create a new Rails app and walk through some tutorials you'll find on the Web. Aaron Bartell has done several of these, as have others. I believe you will find, as I have, that Rails is a cool and productive way to build a Web app on IBM i.

8

PHP on IBM i

Not necessary the "granddaddy" of open source frameworks on IBM i but certainly the most prevalent is PHP. PHP is actually the very first *NIX program I compiled on IBM i. I can't remember the year, it might have been 2004, but I do remember the time of year: it was Thanksgiving, and I was hacking away at PHP and trying to learn how to get stuff to compile in PASE while the turkey was cooking and the family was gathering (pathetic, huh?). Well, you'll be glad to hear that your holidays are safe because PHP has been fully supported on IBM i since around 2006. MySQL was part of the bargain as well, and today the database and PHP live happy lives together in IBM i land. What more could you ask for?

You can dig up the history of PHP on the Internet (you can read Wikipedia as well as I can), but the short story on PHP is that it came into being about the same time as "WWW" was entering the mainstream as a well-known three-letter acronym (TLA). PHP originally was an acronym for Personal Home Page, but better street cred has been gained by using the term: PHP: Hypertext Preprocessor. This is one of the few languages, along with JavaScript, whose original purpose was for the Web. Period. Ruby and Python are scripting languages that have been applied to the Web world, but PHP, along with JavaScript, cut their teeth on the Web. So you'll find a scripting language that is very tightly coupled to HTML. In fact, some of the very early code, and some code you'll find today, has both PHP syntax and HTML in the same file. PHP has matured well past its original HTML and scripting roots to become a stable and well-established object-oriented programming language. You will see all flavors of PHP out there in the wild: from tightly bound script with HTML to MVC implementations with classes and templates. It is a very versatile language.

PHP's organic growth, without benefit of a specification, has led to fits and starts and some naming issues in underlying code. Most of the cruft of evolution has been sorted out. With Unicode support coming as late as 2005, there is still much to do, and PHP is currently at version 7.1 and going strong. Not bad for a language whose author said "I have absolutely no idea how to write a programming language." (Gee, those words could have come from me ....) So let's take a look at this evolving amalgam of scripting language and HTML. We will "take the PHP tour" with a basic grounding in PHP concepts, and then look at how PHP can be used for what it was originally intended: building Web applications.

Where PHP Lives on IBM i

Where does PHP live on IBM i? In PASE, of course! As we discussed in the PASE and ILE chapters, PASE represents an operating system within an operating system: AIX running along and inside of IBM i. Understanding this from a technical standpoint isn't really necessary unless you are a full-fledged propeller-head type, but understanding it from an infrastructure standpoint will help in deployment and configuration.

As you can see from the design in Figure 8.1, Zend Server nestles comfortably within the confines of PASE. It provides the basic infrastructure that retrieves a file from the IFS (a .php file) and processes it with the Zend Server engine—and in this particular case, we have the fastCGI process handling the I/O. fastCGI accelerates the processing of the .php scripts by persisting the application between calls, much like an activation group is used in ILE RPG. Subsequent calls for .php script processing run much more efficiently. Zend Server on IBM i also supports multiple database connectivity options, leveraging much of the Linux, UNIX, and Windows (LUW) world it comes from. Zend (now owned by Rogue Wave Software) has done a great job of bringing the flexibility of the PHP world into the stable world of IBM i, while maintaining great performance.

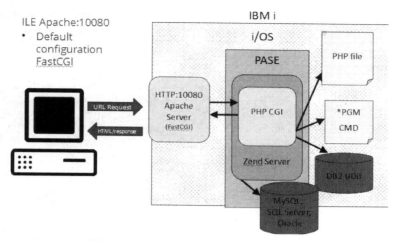

Figure 8.1: Zend Server infrastructure

Installation

I may have had to hack my way through configure scripts in order to get my original install going on my i5 back in 2003, but these days it is *so* much easier. To start with, there isn't anything you *have* to download because your new IBM i will come with a PHP installation available in that vast set of CDs that you regularly ignore as you excitedly unpack the hardware. But rather than rummage for what will probably be a slightly out-of-date copy of PHP, you might as well download the latest and greatest from the Zend website (*www.zend.com*). Look for downloads, and find the download option for IBM i.

As with most things open source on IBM i, you'll need what you probably will see to be the "standard" base licensed programs, shown in Figure 8.2.

```
1.  Portable App Solutions Environment(PASE)   Option 33   Licensed Program 5770SS1
2.  Qshell                                     Option 30   Licensed Program 5770SS1
3.  IBM HTTP Server for i5/OS                   *BASE       Licensed Program 5770DG1
4.  IBM Portable Utilities For I5/OS            *BASE       Licensed Program 5733SC1
5.  OpenSSH, OpenSST, Zlib                      Option 1    Licensed Program 5733SC1
```

Figure 8.2: Base licensed programs for IBM i PHP installation

You probably have these installed. In any case, they are pretty essential to most open source components, but now is a good time to make sure that you are current on Group PTFs. It is always prudent to stay current.

After verifying the existence of your prerequisites, the next step is to unzip and install Zend Server. The instructions at the Zend website should easily get you through the process. It basically boils down to unzipping the file. FTP the file to your IBM, and then run the RSTLICPGM (Restore Licensed Program) command from the save file you FTP'd to the IBM i. Stick it in your library list, and fire it up! Follow the instructions (RTFM is a good step).

Once you have Zend Server installed, you have the power of PHP at your disposal!

Running Scripts

In the short tutorial on PASE in chapter 2, we talked about the *NIX world that PASE lives in, so I am hopeful that you did two things: 1) installed a *real* shell like BASH so you can experience less heartache at the command line and 2) spent some time trying out some of the basic commands to get comfortable with them. For us folks who live on i or in the *NIX world, the command line is where the "coolness" is: "GUI!? We don't need no stinking GUI!" So here is a quick primer on running scripts from the command line.

Don't sweat the difference between using php and php-cli at the command line. Both basically operate the same when invoked in a shell. PHP should already be in your path. You can check that by typing php -v at the command line. I see this:

```
bash-3.00$ php -v
PHP 5.5.20 (cli) (built: Dec 22 2014 17:17:17)
Copyright (c) 1997-2014 The PHP Group
Zend Engine v2.5.0, Copyright (c) 1998-2014 Zend Technologies
```

An additional "smoke test" is to run the which command, which will tell you where the executable lives. My system returns this:

```
bash-3.00$ which php
    /usr/local/zendsvr6/bin/php
```

Cool! Ready to go!

For your own sanity, you will need to locate your command-line scripts in a place that makes some logical sense, so you can find them and run them. My IFS is littered with the flotsam of "good ideas" of where to put stuff—I should have just deleted them because I can no longer find them anyway. More recently, I just started stuffing them into my home folder which, for most user profiles created on IBM i, should be living in the /home folder under the username. So my "home" folder in the IFS is /home/pete, and I automatically end up there when I shell into the IBM i using puTTY. I created a demos folder in that folder, and then I created subfolders in *that* folder for each language. So I have my PHP scripts hanging out in /home/pete/demos/php. When I sign in using puTTY, I end up in /home/pete, so I just cd into the folder I want: cd ~/demos/php (note the tilde "~" is the *NIX shortcut for the home folder). Once I am there, I know that PHP is just waiting for me to run something, so when I want to invoke a script, I simply enter php myscript.php. The output is sent to the terminal.

Programming Basics

At the scripting level, you get just about what you expect. PHP is uses dynamic, untyped variables much like JavaScript, and like JavaScript, you have to indicate when you are using scripting in an HTML page. In JavaScript, you'll have script tags like this: <script> </script>. PHP also has a script tag that begins with <?php and ends with ?>. So in JavaScript, you might see something like this in an HTML page:

```
<script>
console.log "Hello World";
</script>
```

PHP would have something like:

```
<?php
echo "Hello World! ";
?>
```

The two scripts differ in several ways. JavaScript is essentially a client-side script that is interpreted at the browser when included in HTML. PHP scripting is interpreted at the *server*. This is an important distinction. If it is interpreted at the server, then there must be something at the server that can interpret it, and that is usually the PHP binary that runs as a CGI program. So, the two examples show that difference. The JavaScript script outputs to the console; it really has no direct way to write output directly to the browser without manipulating the Document Object Model (DOM). PHP *can* write directly to HTML, and that is handled by the server.

Your PHP scripts will run server-side, and whatever needs to be rendered by the script into HTML is done on the server; then it is all sent to the browser. So, you'll never see the <?php ?> tags in your browser. Those are handled at the server and rendered into HTML, unlike JavaScript, which you *can* view in the browser since it is the browser that interprets the JavaScript. In fact, your PHP code will contain both PHP scripting directives as well as JavaScript, in most cases. That is just fine: two different scripting languages for two different purposes.

The basics of PHP scripting are unsurprising. Outside of getting used to the method for declaring variables, the learning curve should be pretty gentle. Of course, PHP is *way* different from RPG, but some of the language constructs should be relatively easy to wrap your head around.

Variables

The dollar sign ($) indicates the beginning of a variable name in PHP. Beyond that there are some "rules" you'll need to pay attention to:

- A variable name must start with a letter or the underscore character.
- A variable name cannot start with a number.
- A variable name can contain only alphanumeric characters and underscores (A–z, 0–9, and _).
- Variable names are *case-sensitive* ($yeehaw and $YeeHaw are two different variables—yeah, *that* will come back to haunt you at some point).
- Variables declared outside of a function are global.
- Variables declared inside a function are local. You make the local variable "global" by adding the static keyword to the variable declaration. You can access a global variable by using the global keyword within a local function.
- Speaking of "global" variables: those global variables are also accessible in a variable called $GLOBALS, so you can access the values in multiple ways.

Let's put those rules to work, by using a few examples:

```php
<?php
// Comments can be started this way
# Or that way.

//Variables start with $ sign - show me the money!
//Statements end with a semicolon

$greeting = "I'm global";
$x = 5;
$y = 10;

function addme() {
    global $x, $y, $me, $Me;
    $me = "I'm global because I'm declared that way";
    $Me = "I'm different than 'me'";
    $y = $x + $y;
}

function iSay($whatiSay) {
        echo "$whatiSay\r\n";
}

addme();

iSay($greeting);
iSay($y);
iSay($me);
iSay($Me);

?>
```

That is all pretty straightforward. The ability to declare a global variable from within a function is fairly unique and is a good news/bad news kind of thing. Let's say you typically expect your global variables at the top of your script and are reviewing some code where you see what seems to be a global variable further on down the script. Where did it come from? You'll have to search the entire script to determine where it was created. If you are using "include" or "require" to include one .php file in another, it will get even more dicey. If you have many/large scripts in your application, soon it could be out of control. You'll need to be a bit of a "Sherlock" to find it. Thank goodness for search tools! A sane approach would be to design your application up front so that your base globals and functions are located in identifiable files. A little organization goes a long way!

Operators

When it comes to operating on those variables, there isn't much surprising about the ways that you can add, subtract, multiply, and divide in PHP. There are some nice "shortcuts" that you probably recognize, as shown in Table 8.1:

Table 8.1: Math Shortcuts in PHP		
Operation	Expression Example	Shortcut
Assignment	x = y	
Addition	x = x + y	x += y
Subtraction	x = x - y	x -= y
Multiplication	x = x * y	x *= y
Division	x = x/y	x /= y
Modulus	x = x % y	x %= y

Comparison Operators

Again, nothing unusual, especially if you are familiar with JavaScript. The "triple equal" usually throws people for a loop because there really isn't anything like it in RPG. The equal sign (=) is assignment. The double equal sign (==) is a comparison of values. The triple equal sign (===) not only compares the values but also the type of variable. So 1 == 1 is true, and "1" == 1 is true (the character "1" is coerced into an integer). But although 1 ===1 is true, "1" === 1 is false because the types are different (integer vs. string or character). You typically see the triple equal in dynamically typed languages because the values can be coerced to match in some cases, so a "tie-breaking" equal sign needs to be added.

Logical Operators

And and Or are probably second nature to you, but PHP uses double ampersands (&&) and double pipes (||) for "and" and "or," much like JavaScript does. PHP also has an xor operator, which you can use as $x xor $y where either $x or $y can be true, but not both. And, don't forget "not": an exclamation point (!). Forget me not!

Iteration

Yep, PHP has arrays and hashes (associative arrays), just as you would expect. Indexed arrays are pretty much what you'd see declared in other languages. You'd create an array like this:

```
$languages = array("RPG", "Cobol", "Java","PHP","Ruby","Python");
```

To iterate through the array, you might use code like this:

```php
<?php
$languages = array("RPG", "Cobol", "Java","PHP","Ruby","Python");
$ac = count($languages);

    for($x = 0; $x < $ac ; $x++) {
            echo "$languages[$x] is cool\n\r";
}
?>
```

Which would generate:

```
RPG is cool

Cobol is cool

Java is cool

PHP is cool

Ruby is cool

Python is cool
```

Note: The mysterious \n\r at the end of the echo statement is used to add a carriage return \r and line feed \n to each statement, so that it outputs line by line. The teletype still lives!

Associative arrays (hashes) take a slightly different form, using the "hash rocket" notation style seen in other languages:

```
$characters = array("Gandalf"=>"Wizard","Frodo"=>"Hobbit",
"Gimli"=>"Dwarf","Legolas"=>"Elf");
```

You could iterate through the array with a foreach function:

```
foreach($characters as $x => $x_value) {
     // Name = key and role = value
   echo "Name=" . $x . ", role=" . $x_value;
   echo "\n\r";
}
```

The output would be:

```
Name=Gandalf, role=Wizard

Name=Frodo, role=Hobbit

Name=Gimli, role=Dwarf

Name=Legolas, role=Elf
```

Strings

I am going to mention strings here separately and as a transition to a discussion about procedural PHP vs. object-oriented PHP. First things first: strings in PHP can be concatenated easily with a period (.). Typically, in most languages you'd see a plus sign (+) as a concatenation operator when it came to strings, but PHP shows its difference here. So if you had two string variables and wanted to concatenate them, you'd take this approach:

```
$string3 = $string1 . $string2;
```

If you wanted to just append one string to another, you could do it this way:

```
$string1 .= $string2
```

It's one of those "hmmmmm" things that make you wonder why it is defined that way. It's a little more interesting for other string functions, and here is where the difference between a procedural approach and an object-oriented one becomes apparent. There are multiple functions built into PHP for strings. Things like:

strlen   Get the length of a string: $x = strlen("Me") would return 2.

strpos   Get the position *in* a string: $x = strpos("World", "Hello World") would return 6.

str_replace   Find a string and replace it: str_replace("dollar", "cracker", "Polly want a dollar") would result in "Polly want a cracker".

Strings are important in PHP and just about any other language that generates HTML because, well, it's all just text sent out to the browser. You'd expect a text manipulation-intensive language to have some pretty strong string-manipulating capabilities. I barely scratched the surface here. There is much, much more that PHP can do with text data. But PHP can be used procedurally as well as in an object-oriented way. Before you get too excited, though, strings aren't objects in PHP. You can't do this, for example:

```
$myname = "Thorin Oakenshield";

$myname->length
```

and get 18 returned. You'd still have to use strlen($myname). Even if you built an object like this:

```php
<?php

class Person{

        public $myname = "Thorin Oakenshield";
}

$me = new Person();

echo "$me->myname\r\n";

$me->myname = "Gandalf Greyhame";

echo $me->myname;

?>
```

With output of:

```
Thorin Oakenshield
Gandalf Greyhame
```

there wouldn't be a length property unless you specifically added it. You'd still have to use the strlen($me->myname) syntax to get the length of the string. There are libraries you can download that will add more object-oriented capabilities to strings, but out of the box, you are still going to use the "old" procedural built-in functions to manipulate strings. It's not a huge deal, but if you come from an object-oriented world, your expectations might be a bit different from reality.

Accessing System Resources

Files

File access, such as creating, deleting, reading, and writing to the IFS, can be done directly from a PHP script using the native file system APIs. We are in *NIX land, so we'll be using very *NIX-like API calls to get there. Here's a simple example:

```php
<?php
$myfile = fopen("demofile.txt", "w") or die("Unable to open file!");
$txt = "I love PHP! \n";
fwrite($myfile, $txt);
$txt = "I love PASE!\n";
fwrite($myfile, $txt);
$txt = "I love IBM i!\n";
fwrite($myfile, $txt);

fclose($myfile);

$myfile = fopen("demofile.txt", "r") or die("Unable to open file!");
// Output one line until end-of-file
while(!feof($myfile)) {
   echo fgets($myfile);
}

fclose($myfile);
?>
```

We open the file for writing and then, line by line, write to it. Then we close it and reopen it, and then output the contents. Pretty straightforward.

Running System Commands

As in the other chapters, we really are looking at a couple of different angles on the "system resources" puzzle. The most obvious is getting to the hosting OS, which will be PASE because, as we quickly reviewed at the beginning of this chapter, PHP runs in PASE. There are three options, which are all very similar but have different use cases:

exec—This will run the command in PASE and then return. If the command returns output, you will need to access the output and do whatever it is you need to do yourself. Nothing will be "automatically" returned to the PHP script, whether or not output is generated.

system—This will run the command, and if there is output to be returned, it will return it. So, for example, if you ran this script:

```php
<?php
 system("ls -l ~")
?>
```

The script would list the files in your home directory and return the list back to the calling script. Run from the command line, I get my list of files returned to the command line.

passthru—Nearly identical to "system" when run in PASE, it can also return raw, binary data.

Note also that the previous example that used the file APIs accessed files from the hosting OS level, which is PASE, so all "system" file access in PASE is getting to the IFS.

This is all fine and dandy, but in most cases, you'll want to go deeper, lower, and access IBM i resources. Let's take a look at how to do that.

Database Access

Accessing a database takes a little more work than just accessing the IFS because database access isn't a trivial matter. In DB2 for i, we have all manner of tables and files, so you may need to do some research if you are still running multi-membered files. The examples here are geared toward SQL access rather than RLA, which may throw you as well. (Get used to it! SQL is cool.) Comments are in the code.

```php
<?php
// Since we are connecting to IBM i (running the script from PASE),
// there is already a "connection" that IBM i will recognize.
// It will use the user profile that your PASE connection uses.
// Override it if need be.

$conn_resource = db2_connect("*LOCAL", "", "");
```

Continued

```php
// display the error if something falls over
if (!$conn_resource) {
    echo "Connection failed. SQL Err:";
    echo db2_conn_error();
    echo " \n\r";
    echo db2_conn_errormsg();

exit();
}
/* Construct the SQL statement */
// There is a simple employee table I created that I use for demos.
// No REAL data here
$sql = "SELECT * FROM EMPLOYEE.EMPLOYEE ORDER BY EMPLNAME,EMPFNAME FOR
FETCH ONLY";

/* Prepare and execute the DB2 SQL statement */
$stmt= db2_prepare($conn_resource, $sql);

// Run the statement
$result = db2_execute($stmt);

    if (!$result) { /* again, check for errors */
        echo 'The db2 execute failed. ';
        echo 'SQLSTATE value: ' . db2_stmt_error();
        echo ' Message: ' .   db2_stmt_errormsg();
    }
    else
    {
        // Statement must have been OK. Iterate through the results
        // Each $row that is fetched is an array of columns from
        // your select statement
        while ($row = db2_fetch_array($stmt))
          {
                echo "$row[1]  $row[2]  $row[3] \n\r";
```

Continued

```
                }
            }
        // The connection automagically closes when the script completes
?>
```

Whether the SQL is used to read or write, the steps are basically the same. We could insert records using syntax similar to this:

```
$sql = "INSERT INTO Employee.employee (empfname, emplname, empemail)
VALUES (?, ?, ?)";

$stmt= db2_prepare($conn_resource, $sql);

db2_bind_param($prepare, 1, "firstname", DB2_PARAM_IN);
db2_bind_param($prepare, 2, "lastname", DB2_PARAM_IN);
db2_bind_param($prepare, 3, "email", DB2_PARAM_IN);
```

And then we would set our parameters and update:

```
$firstname = "Joe";
$lastname = "Zablotnick";
$email = "joe_z@example.com";

db2_execute($stmt);
```

Pretty simple. The *one* thing to pay attention to, and what tripped me up, is that when I explicitly bound the parameters, I used the variable names *without* the leading $ in the bind statements but still used the variable names with the $ when I assigned values to them before execution.

Running the code in the example that uses the SELECT statement after I inserted the "Zablotnick" record, renders this:

```
Admin   Administrator  12345 Mainly Street
Peekop  Andropoff   444 East St
```

```
Charlie  BesterTester  1234 Ash
Nuthin  Doing  156 Main
Seeme  Going  12 East Oak
Maybe  Later  123 East Main
Andy  Rooney  111 Sin Street
Joe  Zablotnick
```

I'll never make a living as a DBA.

Accessing IBM i Commands and Programs

In addition to database access, you'll perhaps want to access commands or programs in the IBM "native" world. Whenever you think about crossing the PASE/IBM i boundary, your first thought should be XMLSERVICE, the "Swiss Army Knife" of crossing the PASE border. PHP is no different when it comes to using XMLSERVICE resources, but there have been a few iterations on the PHP side of the house when it comes to the "toolkit." Initially there was the Easycom toolkit from Aura, which came to end of life at the end of 2011. In order to preserve some of the code that leveraged the "old" toolkit, there was a "compatibility wrapper" that used the clever acronym of CW. These days it is just the PHP toolkit. You'll find it in the ToolkitAPI folder of your zendsvr installation. My recommendation is that you avoid any examples that contain the old "i5_" functions (and there are a lot of them). The new API is more object-oriented and more compact and, I think, easier to understand. I guess you'll be the judge.

The PHP toolkit is really just making calls to XMLSERVICE using PHP scripting. That is the cool thing about XMLSERVICE. So, if you have dragged yourself through other examples I provided in other languages, then you'll be in familiar territory here.

Simple Commands

Here is an example of just running a simple command using the toolkit:

```php
<?php

include_once 'authorization.php';

include_once 'ToolkitService.php';
```
Continued

```php
try {

$obj = ToolkitService::getInstance($db, $user, $pass);

}

catch (Exception $e) {

        echo $e->getMessage(), "\n";

        exit();

}


$obj->setToolkitServiceParams(array('InternalKey'=>"/tmp/$user",

                                    'debug'=>true,

                                    'plug' => "iPLUG32K"));

$cmd = "addlible ZENDSVR6";

$obj->CLCommand($cmd);

$Rows = $obj->CLInteractiveCommand("DSPLIBL");

/*$Rows = $obj->CLInteractiveCommand("WRKSYSVAL
OUTPUT(*PRINT)");*/

if(!$Rows )

        echo $obj->getLastError();

else
        foreach($Rows as $row) {
                echo $row."\r\n";
        }
```

Continued

```
        //var_dump($Rows);

        /* Do not use the disconnect() function for "stateful" connection
*/

        $obj->disconnect();

?>
```

So we start with a couple of includes. The first, and for me the most mysterious, was the authorization.php file. Although I saw this file referenced in many demos, there was no mention of what it contained or where it was found. So let me tell you what I did: I created the file in the same directory as my demo files, and it contains the $db, $user, and $pass variable values. My authorization.php file ended up looking like this:

```
<?php
$db = "*LOCAL";
$user = "";
$pass = "";
$internalKey = "/tmp/$user";
$libxmlservice = "XMLSERVICE";
?>
```

(More about the last two variables later.)

The other include file, ToolkitService.php, lives in the /usr/local/zendsvr6/share/ ToolkitAPI folder—at least it does on my 7.2 partition. It contains the "wrapper" code that marshals the data into and out from the XMLSERVICE library on IBM i.

The next section of code:

```
    try {

            $obj = ToolkitService::getInstance($db, $user, $pass);

                                                            Continued
```

```
    }

    catch (Exception $e) {

        echo $e->getMessage(), "\n";

        exit();

    }
```

is that cooler, more object-oriented stuff I talked about. The getInstance method, which is called statically from the ToolkitService class, is passed a database reference along with the user and password for the connection. In this case, I used *LOCAL as the database because the connection was local: I was connecting through the PASE world into the IBM i world, and I was using my IBM i user profile to do so. You could easily override the database, user, and password values if you needed to (hence the beauty of having it in a separate file). That getInstance method returns a ToolkitService object, which has a bunch of useful methods (functions) that can be invoked.

The try/catch method is a common error-handling approach that also applies to PHP. If the call to getInstance fails for some reason, then the catch block is used to process the failure. In this case, a failure leads to a "blarg and bail," which in my vernacular is dump out the error message and exit the program.

The next section does the "heavy lifting":

```
    $obj->setToolkitServiceParams(array('InternalKey'=>"/tmp/$user",

                                        'debug'=>true,

                                        'plug' => "iPLUG32K"));

    $cmd = "addlible ZENDSVR6";

    $obj->CLCommand($cmd);

    $Rows = $obj->CLInteractiveCommand("DSPLIBL");
```

XMLSERVICE needs some parameters, so we stuff them into an array and call the setToolkitServiceParams method to set them. Next, we see a couple of different implementations of CL invocation. The first one, which is the addlible command, adds the ZENDSVR library to the library list. That's it. Nothing is returned. The second invocation, the DISPLIBL, is invoked using the "interactive" option, and it assumes that something *will* be returned—in this case, the listing of DISPLIBL. That content is returned to another variable called $Rows, which, if you know what a DISPLIBL to *PRINT—DSPLIBL OUTPUT(*PRINT)—does, you probably guessed that $Rows is an array of print lines from the output of the command. Right you are!

What do you do with an array of data? You iterate through it! (Almost sounds illegal.) Let's do it:

```
if(!$Rows )

        echo $obj->getLastError();

else

        foreach($Rows as $row) {
                echo $row."\r\n";
        }

        //var_dump($Rows);

        /* Do not use the disconnect() function for "stateful" connection
*/

        $obj->disconnect();
```

If we didn't end up with any $Rows, we do a quick reality check to see if there is an error lurking. If we have more than 0 rows, then we do a foreach iteration through the array, grabbing a row of output at a time. Then we disconnect ($obj->disconnect();) from the IBM i to release resources. On my system, the results looked like this:

```
5770SS1 V7R2M0   140418                        Library List
9/10/16 10:56:21              Page    1
                                      ASP
    Library       Type          Device        Text Description
    QSYS          SYS                         System Library
    QSYS2         SYS                         System Library for CPI's
    QHLPSYS       SYS
    QUSRSYS       SYS                         System Library for Users
    ZENDSVR       USR
    QGPL          USR                         General Purpose Library
    QTEMP         USR
 * * * * *  E N D   O F   L I S T I N G  * * * * *
```

Clearly it is a *PRINT of output from a spooled file.

I normally would remove // comments from a demo unless I had a reason to leave them in. In this case, I do have a reason. Uncomment the line that has:

```
/*$Rows = $obj->CLInteractiveCommand("WRKSYSVAL OUTPUT(*PRINT)");*/
```

by removing the /* and the closing */, and just comment out the $Rows = $obj->CLInteractiveCommand("DSPLIBL"); with a double forward slash:

```
//$Rows = $obj->CLInteractiveCommand("DSPLIBL");
```

Save and rerun your code, and you'll get a boatload of output (if you have access to the command). You may want to output the contents to a file instead of terminal, so we can combine the earlier demo on IFS file access with this one and dump the contents to a file in the IFS. That "combo" would look like this small modification:

```
// Open the file
      $myfile = fopen("demofile.txt", "w") or die("Unable to open
file!");
```
Continued

```
    if(!$Rows )

        echo $obj->getLastError();

    else
        foreach($Rows as $row) {
            // write to the file

            fwrite($myfile, $row."\r\n");

        }
    // close the file
    fclose($myfile);
```

It's just drop-dead simple to change to file output.

The other item that was commented out was the var_dump (not a very attractive method). var_dump can be used to get the data from a variable delivered in "raw" form. You'll see it sometimes for debugging and sometimes for just a quick and dirty (Q&D) display of data. In our case, foreach is the perfect way to get the data returned from the calling method.

Calling Programs and Procedures

Yeah, you can do calls to programs and procedures as well; it is just, ahem, a *little* more involved. Let's think about it for a second: you are in the PHP environment that really doesn't give a rip about what you have cleverly stuffed into your variables, and you are going to call an RPG program or procedure that is *very* picky about what you pass to it. This is the "Odd Couple" sitcom of programming: a very messy PHP living side by side with an anal retentive, neat freak RPG.

The differences are arbitrated by specifying exactly what goes in and what comes out. The section on XMLSERVICE covered this, and there is plenty of documentation on how to specify data types in XMLSERVICE. The PHP toolkit has to play by these rules. So, you can imagine that all of this detail is going to add some verbosity to our call to RPG. Your imagination is correct. Hang on to your coffee cup; here is an example:

```php
<?php
include_once 'authorization.php';

include_once 'ToolkitService.php';

//The ToolkitService connection method/function uses either IBM_
//DB2 (default) or ODBC extensions to connect
//to IBM i server. In order to switch to an ODBC connection, assign an
//"odbc" value to the $extension variable
//and make sure that the ODBC extension is enabled in the PHP.INI file.
//The ODBC extension usage in ToolkitService is preferable in 2-tier
//environment: Zend Server running in Windows/Linux
//and accessing database and/or programs in IBM i server

$extension='ibm_db2';

try { $ToolkitServiceObj = ToolkitService::getInstance($db, $user,
$pass, $extension); }
catch (Exception $e) { die($e->getMessage()); }

$ToolkitServiceObj->setToolkitServiceParams(
array('InternalKey'=>$internalKey, // route to same XMLSERVICE job
                                   // /tmp/myjob1
'subsystem'=>"QGPL/QDFTJOBD",      // subsystem/jobd to start XMLSERVICE
                                   // (if not running)
'plug'=>"iPLUG32K"));              // max size data i/o (iPLUG4K,
                                   // 32K,65K,512K,1M,5M,10M,15M)

//     D  INCHARA        S           1a
//     D  INCHARB        S           1a
//     D  INDEC1         S           7p 4
//     D  INDEC2         S           12p 2
//     D  INDS1          DS
//     D   DSCHARA                   1a
//     D   DSCHARB                   1a
//     D   DSDEC1                    7p 4
```

Continued

```
//      D   DSDEC2                       12p 2
//       *+++++++++++++++++++++++++++++++++++++++++++++++++++++++++++++++
//       * main(): Control flow
//       *+++++++++++++++++++++++++++++++++++++++++++++++++++++++++++++++
//      C        *Entry       PLIST
//      C                     PARM                        INCHARA
//      C                     PARM                        INCHARB
//      C                     PARM                        INDEC1
//      C                     PARM                        INDEC2
//      C                     PARM                        INDS1
```

```php
$param[] = $ToolkitServiceObj->AddParameterChar    ('both', 1, 'INCHARA',
'var1', 'Y');

$param[] = $ToolkitServiceObj->AddParameterChar    ('both', 1, 'INCHARB',
'var2', 'Z');

$param[] = $ToolkitServiceObj->AddParameterPackDec('both', 7,4,'INDEC1',
'var3', '001.0001');

$param[] = $ToolkitServiceObj->AddParameterPackDec('both', 12,2,
'INDEC2', 'var4', '0000000003.04');

   $ds[] = $ToolkitServiceObj->AddParameterChar    ('both', 1, 'DSCHA-
RA', 'ds1', 'A');

   $ds[] = $ToolkitServiceObj->AddParameterChar    ('both', 1,
'DSCHARB', 'ds2', 'B');

   $ds[] = $ToolkitServiceObj->AddParameterPackDec('both', 7,4,'DSDEC1',
'ds3', '005.0007');

   $ds[] = $ToolkitServiceObj->AddParameterPackDec('both', 12,2,
'DSDEC1', 'ds4', '0000000006.08');

$param[] = $ToolkitServiceObj->AddDataStruct($ds);

$result  = $ToolkitServiceObj->PgmCall('ZZCALL', $libxmlservice, $param,
null, null);

// simple dump output
var_dump($result);

// Do not use the disconnect() function for "state full" connection
$ToolkitServiceObj->disconnect();
?>
```

COWABUNGA! This example from the Young i Professionals (YiPs) website (*yips .idevcloud.com/wiki*) is busy because we also included a snippet from the RPG program being called, so we can see what is being passed and why. If you downloaded and installed XMLSERVICE from GitHub or the YiPs website, you'll have all the RPG code that is being called by the examples. It can help you understand things a bit more completely. In this case, the RPG code that isn't displayed as part of the documentation in the PHP script is this:

```
/free
  Step +=1;
  INCHARA = 'C';
  INCHARB = 'D';
  INDEC1 = 321.1234;
  INDEC2 = 1234567890.12;
  DSCHARA = 'E';
  DSCHARB = 'F';
  DSDEC1 = 333.333;
  DSDEC2 = 4444444444.44;
  return;
  // *inlr = *on;
/end-free
```

OK, that isn't the most elegant code, but it demonstrates the essentials of this example, and that is that there are values passed in and values passed out that can be handled by the toolkit, regardless of what they are. We have individual values and a data structure passed in and returned. Most of your programs will have some variation of that. And if your code is currently in a more modular form, that code is ready to be used by PHP! Simple! You can also see in the example how values are passed from PHP to RPG. The line

```
"$param[] = $ToolkitServiceObj->AddParameterChar  ('both', 1,
  'INCHARA', 'var1', 'Y');"
```

shows you what is needed: 'both' defining the parameter as both input and output, 1 defining the length of the parameter, 'INCHARA' as the RPG variable name, 'var1' as the PHP variable name, and 'Y' as the actual *value* of the variable that is passed.

Each parameter that is passed needs to be defined in that way. Again, check the YiPs website and look for "data types" in the XMLSERVICE section.

Here is the (somewhat predicable) output:

```
array(2) {
  ["io_param"]=>
  array(5) {
    ["var1"]=>
    string(1) "C"
    ["var2"]=>
    string(1) "D"
    ["var3"]=>
    string(8) "321.1234"
    ["var4"]=>
    string(13) "1234567890.12"
    ["struct_name"]=>
    array(4) {
      ["ds1"]=>
      string(1) "E"
      ["ds2"]=>
      string(1) "F"
      ["ds3"]=>
      string(8) "333.3330"
      ["ds4"]=>
      string(13) "4444444444.44"
    }
  }
  ["retvals"]=>
  array(0) {
  }
}
```

Your thought is probably "Dude! That is, like, the UGLIEST thing I have ever seen!" I agree. But I also "dumped" (if you'll pardon the expression), which is why you are seeing stuff in the output that is equally verbose as to what went in. var_dump just dumps the structure and data in raw form as output. So we are seeing the nested structure and types of the parameters along with the data. Again, for Q&D output and debugging, var_dump can be useful, but in most cases you'll use either iteration to walk the output *or* directly reference it with something like this:

```
echo $result["io_param"]["struct_name"]["ds4"];
```

Which would output 4444444444.44.

PHP in the Web World

The command-line stuff is cool, but PHP was built for the Web, so how do we make this stuff "webby"? HTML is just text, folks, so we are almost there because these examples output text. But, in order to get there, we need to take a step back and reorient ourselves to the way a Web server works. As the illustration at the beginning of this chapter showed, a request from a browser comes in to the Apache server, and the content is evaluated to determine how it should be handled. A request for an HTML page will directly return the HTML because a browser knows what to do with it. But if the request is for a PHP file, then the contents of the PHP file need to be processed into HTML first, then returned. That is where the PHP-CGI module comes into play. Apache basically hands off the file to PHP-CGI and says "Hey, *you* handle this and return me HTML." We actually have already seen this in action in a limited way from the command line. Basically when we run php myfile.php, we tell the PHP binary to process the PHP file and do whatever it is supposed to. The examples we have run so far have mostly returned text to the command shell.

The PHP-CGI magic happens in the Apache (HTTP) Web server on IBM i. We use unique directives to tell Apache how to handle a PHP file like so:

Load up the Zend PHP server programs:

```
LoadModule proxy_module /QSYS.LIB/QHTTPSVR.LIB/QZSRCORE.SRVPGM
LoadModule proxy_http_module /QSYS.LIB/QHTTPSVR.LIB/QZSRCORE.SRVPGM
LoadModule proxy_connect_module /QSYS.LIB/QHTTPSVR.LIB/QZSRCORE.SRVPGM
LoadModule proxy_ftp_module /QSYS.LIB/QHTTPSVR.LIB/QZSRCORE.SRVPGM
LoadModule proxy_balancer_module /QSYS.LIB/QHTTPSVR.LIB/QZSRCORE.SRVPGM
LoadModule zend_enabler_module /QSYS.LIB/QHTTPSVR.LIB/QZFAST.SRVPGM
```

Invoke the fastcgi method when processing a file with a .php extension, and recognize the php MIME type:

```
AddType application/x-httpd-php .php .php5
AddHandler fastcgi-script .php .php5
```

These are the only directives you need to *add* when you create a new configuration file in Apache. The Create HTTP Server wizard in the HTTP admin console will create the base file, then go ahead and add the directives above. The whole tamale will look like this:

```
# Configuration originally created by Create HTTP Server wizard on Sat
Sep 10 14:15:46 CDT 2016
LoadModule proxy_module /QSYS.LIB/QHTTPSVR.LIB/QZSRCORE.SRVPGM
LoadModule proxy_http_module /QSYS.LIB/QHTTPSVR.LIB/QZSRCORE.SRVPGM
LoadModule proxy_connect_module /QSYS.LIB/QHTTPSVR.LIB/QZSRCORE.SRVPGM
LoadModule proxy_ftp_module /QSYS.LIB/QHTTPSVR.LIB/QZSRCORE.SRVPGM
LoadModule proxy_balancer_module /QSYS.LIB/QHTTPSVR.LIB/QZSRCORE.SRVPGM
LoadModule zend_enabler_module /QSYS.LIB/QHTTPSVR.LIB/QZFAST.SRVPGM

Listen 10.0.10.205:5555

DocumentRoot /www/phpdemo/htdocs
TraceEnable Off
Options -FollowSymLinks
LogFormat "%h %T %l %u %t \"%r\" %>s %b \"%{Referer}i\" \"%{User-Agent}
i\"" combined
LogFormat "%{Cookie}n \"%r\" %t" cookie
LogFormat "%{User-agent}i" agent
LogFormat "%{Referer}i -> %U" referer
LogFormat "%h %l %u %t \"%r\" %>s %b" common
CustomLog logs/access_log combined
LogMaint logs/access_log 7 0
LogMaint logs/error_log 7 0
                                                      Continued
```

```
SetEnvIf "User-Agent" "Mozilla/2" nokeepalive
SetEnvIf "User-Agent" "JDK/1\.0" force-response-1.0
SetEnvIf "User-Agent" "Java/1\.0" force-response-1.0
SetEnvIf "User-Agent" "RealPlayer 4\.0" force-response-1.0
SetEnvIf "User-Agent" "MSIE 4\.0b2;" nokeepalive
SetEnvIf "User-Agent" "MSIE 4\.0b2;" force-response-1.0

# zend fastcgi
AddType application/x-httpd-php .php .php5
AddHandler fastcgi-script .php .php5

<Directory />
   Require all denied
</Directory>
<Directory /www/phpdemo/htdocs>
   Require all granted
</Directory>
```

If you *are* going to use fastcgi, then make sure you have a copy of the fastcgi.conf file in the conf folder of your app that the Create HTTP Server wizard creates. You should have a fastcgi.conf file in your /www/zendsvr6/conf folder in the IFS. Just copy that over to your app folder.

You drop your .php files into the document root (/www/phpdemo/htdocs in this example). So, let's circle back around to our command-line demos and make them more "webby." The things that most of the command-line examples are missing are the HTML directives and tags that will make the output look less text-ty and more sexy in a browser. Standard HTML usually has this:

```
<!DOCTYPE html>
<html>
  <head>
    <title>My web page</title>
```
Continued

```
        <meta name="content-type" content="text/html; charset=ISO-8859-1">
        <!--The file may or may not have stylesheets to format the html-->
        <!--<link rel="stylesheet" type="text/css" href="./styles.css">-->
        <!--The file may or may not have javascript to manipulate the DOM and
the output-->
        <!--<script src="./somescript.js">-->
    </head>

    <body>
      This is my HTML page. <br>
    </body>
</html>
```

You'll put your PHP stuff in between the <body></body> tags in your HTML document. Let's go back to our simple file I/O example and put that into our handy-dandy HTML document and run it. Simply copying and pasting it into the HTML is enough, really! The resulting file would look like this:

```
<!DOCTYPE html>
<html>
  <head>
    <title>Demo of simple file I/O - web version</title>
    <meta name="content-type" content="text/html; charset=ISO-8859-1">
    <!--The file may or may not have stylesheets to format the html-->
    <!--<link rel="stylesheet" type="text/css" href="./styles.css">-->
    <!--The file may or may not have javascript to manipulate the DOM and
the output-->
    <!--<script src="./somescript.js">-->
  </head>
  <body>
  <h1>Demo of simple file I/O - web version</h1>
  <?php
      $myfile = fopen("demofile.txt", "w") or die("Unable to open file
for writing!");
```

Continued

```
        $txt = "I love PHP! \n";
        fwrite($myfile, $txt);
        $txt = "I love PASE!\n";
        fwrite($myfile, $txt);
        $txt = "I love IBM i!\n";
        fwrite($myfile, $txt);

        fclose($myfile);

        $myfile = fopen("demofile.txt", "r") or die("Unable to open file
for reading!");
        // Output one line until end-of-file
        while(!feof($myfile)) {
          echo fgets($myfile)."<br>";
        }

        fclose($myfile);
?>
    </body>
</html>
```

Hopefully you recognize the code between the <?php?> markers as the code we ran before. *Disclosure*: Normally you wouldn't be able to run code like this because it requires WRITE permission in the htdocs folder which, if granted, should make anyone squeamish about security. So *if* you decide to give this a whirl on your server and you *do* grant WRITE permission to the htdocs folder (as I have for this demo), then either keep that server instance off the Internet (as I have) *or* remove the WRITE permissions once you have played with it.

My only modification to the original PHP code was to add the <br> to the output statement.
 is equivalent to the "newline" characters we used before. That's it! Again, this is a "dangerous" example because of the write permissions needed, but if you were just reading a file in the IFS and outputting the contents to the browser, standard read permissions will work just fine.

The SQL I/O would look like this:

```
<!DOCTYPE html>
<html>
  <head>
    <title>SQL access demo web</title>
    <meta name="content-type" content="text/html; charset=ISO-8859-1">
    <!--The file may or may not have stylesheets to format the html-->
    <!--<link rel="stylesheet" type="text/css" href="./styles.css">-->
    <!--The file may or may not have javascript to manipulate the DOM and
the output-->
    <!--<script src="./somescript.js">-->
  </head>

  <body>
  <h1>SQL access demo web</h1>
  <br>
<?php
$conn_resource = db2_connect("*LOCAL", "", "");

if (!$conn_resource) {
    echo "Connection failed. SQL Err:";
    echo db2_conn_error();
    echo "<br>";
    echo db2_conn_errormsg();

exit();
}
/* Construct the SQL statement */
$sql = "SELECT * FROM EMPLOYEE.EMPLOYEE ORDER BY EMPLNAME,EMPFNAME FOR
FETCH ONLY";

/* Prepare and execute the DB2 SQL statement */
$stmt= db2_prepare($conn_resource, $sql);
```
                                                                    Continued

```
$result = db2_execute($stmt);

     if (!$result) {
         echo 'The db2 execute failed. ';
         echo 'SQLSTATE value: ' . db2_stmt_error();
         echo ' Message: ' .   db2_stmt_errormsg();
     }
     else
     {
       while ($row = db2_fetch_array($stmt))
       {
       echo "$row[1]   $row[2]   $row[3] <br>";
       }
     }
?>
   </body>
</html>
```

And again, the only tweak to the whole process was adding the <br> tag for each line.

I bet you can figure out how to include the code for the simple command call we made in an earlier example. You can copy and paste stuff as easily as I can. Just remember to replace the \n\r with <br> so you get line-by-line access.

I hope this chapter helped you see how easy and versatile PHP is. Of all the languages discussed in this book, PHP may well be the easiest to get started with if your focus is the Web.

A bit of wisdom: "Now the serpent was more crafty than any of the wild animals the LORD God had made." (Gen. 3:1)

9

Python

Finally, a language name that you can love! Although a snake is the logo for Python, it should really be a "flying circus" logo since the origin of the name is rumored to be based on *Monty Python's Flying Circus*, the awesome, irreverent British comedy of the early 1970s. "And now for something completely different."

Python began as a scripting language developed by Guido van Rossum. In its current form, it has both procedural and object-oriented (OO) capabilities. Its procedural bent should make it easy for RPG programmers to transition to the language.

The focus of the language is to provide simple syntax, performance, and extensibility, and it delivers on all three. Although not as well-known as Ruby or PHP, it has been around since 1989, so it could be considered the mature older brother of many popular scripting languages today. Guido (love the name) continues to oversee the language, as he has been designated as the BDFL (benevolent dictator for life).

Even though Python is a "scripting" language, it is usually compiled down to bytecode to increase execution speed, and often the extensions are native to the OS it is running on. Since it has been around a while, is easy to comprehend, and is a versatile scripting language, you'll find Python everywhere. It is literally "out of this world" in that NASA uses Python extensively in its systems (along with C) because of the lightweight, performant, and easy-to-learn nature of the language. So how easy is it? And now for something completely different.

It's "Hello World" again.

```
print "Hello World"
```

Simple. Nice. We know what print does.

The purpose of this chapter is to get you grounded in Python. We take a tour of installation, invocation, language syntax details, objects, methods, functions, and a whole lot more. There is much to like in the Python world.

Installation

Before we jump headlong into writing code, we should probably get Python installed! Like most open source languages, Python has a few "flavors" out there, and the folks on IBM i will appreciate the fact that one version has maintained some extensive backward compatibility (not quite like IBM i but not bad), and the "latest" version hasn't. So you'll need to decide if you want to install version 2 of Python or version 3.

Version 2 was delivered in October 2000, and Version 3 was delivered in December 2008. Version 3, despite much gnashing of teeth, is not backward compatible. The code base for version 2 is quite extensive and in most cases will not run with version 3. The biggest change from version 2 to version 3 was the cleanup of redundant code and functions, the implementing of print as function, and the use of Unicode for strings. There is a tool 2to3 that can convert most of the Python 2 code to Python 3 code. I'd recommend you install both versions so that you can run code from either version if needed. The code bases didn't stagnate, by the way. There has been plenty of activity in the Python 2 track and the Python 3 track. Python 2 is at version 2.7, and Python 3 is at version 3.5, and of course there are incremental updates as well. IBM i currently installs version 2.7.11 and/ or version 3.4.4.

How to install? Python has long been a staple on IBM i in an incarnation called iSeriesPython that currently supports Python version 2.7. But as part of IBM's Open

Source Initiative, there is now a licensed product that installs pretty much all the currently supported open source programs on IBM i. You install it by installing licensed program 5733OPS using the Install Licensed Program option on the Licensed Program menu (option 11).

Install Licensed Programs will take care of the install if you don't have the IBM i Open Source product installed. If you *do* already have the licensed program installed, then ordering the Group PTF for 5733OPS will get the latest and greatest version of code installed. If all goes well, you should be able to start a terminal session in the PASE environment, type python2 -V and python3 -V, and see the following:

```
bash-3.00$ python2 -V
Python 2.7.11
bash-3.00$ python3 -V
Python 3.4.4
```

Of course, your versions may well be different than those listed above because the "march of the open source versions" will continue unabated for the foreseeable future.

I made the installation a little bit easier than it often is in reality. There are a few good resources available. Your first stop should be the IBM developerWorks website, specifically (as of this writing) *https://www.ibm.com/developerworks/community/wikis/ home?lang=en#!/wiki/IBM%20i%20Technology%20Updates*. You can check the open source pages at *common.org* or the mailing list at *midrange.com*. And you can always check my blog (*www.petesworkshop.com/blog_wp*) since I try to keep up with the latest in the IBM i arena.

Programming in Python

Python pretty much follows the usual programming paradigms that we are all familiar with. It has all the variable assignment stuff you would expect, and it has five very basic data types.

Numbers

No big surprises here except for "complex" numbers that, frankly, I don't understand. You math geeks may be encouraged by the presence of a complex number, but, well, I haven't used them. But integers, longs, and floats I understand.

Strings

A string is, well, a string of characters enclosed by single or double quotes. As in other object-oriented languages, a string is an object and will have several useful methods already defined for it. Things like find, upper, and lower do what you think they do:

```
myName= "Pete HelgreN"
offset = myName.find('gr')
print offset
print myName.upper()
print myName.lower()
print myName.title()
```

The output would be:

```
8
PETE HELGREN
pete helgren
Pete Helgren
```

Lists

This is much like an array: just a list of items in what I would call a traditional array syntax. It looks like this:

```
languages = ['Python','Ruby','JavaScript',42, 77.5]
```

OK, the last two entries weren't programming languages, but what I wanted to demonstrate was that the values can be basically anything. And, since the list data type is an object, you can expect that there would be useful built-in functions. And there are! Like these:

```
languages = ['Python','Ruby','JavaScript',42, 77.5]

print languages[2]
print languages
languages.insert(3,'PHP')
print languages
languages.remove(42)
print languages
languages.reverse()
print languages
```

The output would be:

```
JavaScript
['Python', 'Ruby', 'JavaScript', 42, 77.5]
['Python', 'Ruby', 'JavaScript', 'PHP', 42, 77.5]
['Python', 'Ruby', 'JavaScript', 'PHP', 77.5]
[77.5, 'PHP', 'JavaScript', 'Ruby', 'Python']
```

Tuples

Math geeks will already know what a "tuple" is, but for the benefit of those of us who live on planet Earth and will be writing Python code, a tuple is a series of immutable Python objects. Much like traditional arrays and lists in Python, tuples are sequences. The difference between tuples and lists is the tuples cannot be changed (immutable, remember?). Also unlike lists, tuples use parentheses instead of the square brackets. One other thing: if you build a list of items without putting parentheses or square brackets around them, the assumption is that they are a tuple. So this:

```
languages = ('Python','Ruby','JavaScript',42, 77.5)
```

would be the same as this:

```
languages = 'Python','Ruby','JavaScript',42, 77.5
```

Let's try some things on for size because tuples are also objects and will have some built-in methods:

Will this work?

```
languages = ('Python','Ruby','JavaScript',42, 77.5)
print languages
languages[3]= "PHP"
```

Nope!

```
line 3, in <module>
    'Python', 'Ruby', 'JavaScript', 42, 77.5)
languages[3]= "PHP"
TypeError: 'tuple' object does not support item assignment
```

Maybe a slightly different assignment?

```
languages = 'Python','Ruby','JavaScript',42, 77.5
print languages
languages[3]= "PHP"
```

Nope! It's a tuple by default:

```
line 3, in <module>
    languages[3]= "PHP"
TypeError: 'tuple' object does not support item assignment
```

There are plenty of nice functions available to us.

```
languages = 'Python','Ruby','JavaScript',42, 77.5
print languages
                                                    Continued
```

```
print languages[2]
print languages[-2]

for x in languages: print x
```

The last example is useful because it can be used with lists as well. We haven't jumped into full programming in Python yet, but like many other languages, iteration is a foundational building block.

Dictionary

A dictionary is a sequence of name-value pairs. Similar to hashes in other languages, a dictionary can be used to "look up" one value with another. Anyone who has worked with JavaScript objects, particularly with JSON strings, would be comfortable with the concept of a dictionary. However, you can use both numbers and strings or really any valid data type for "name." Any object can be used as a value. Take a look at the following:

```
dict = {}
dict['one'] = "The loneliest number"
dict[42]    = "This is the meaning of life"
print dict
```

The output would be:

```
{42: 'This is the meaning of life', 'one': 'The loneliest number'}
```

print dict[42] would output "This is the meaning of life", and if we accidentally used the same name to assign a value later, we would basically be reassigning the value:

```
dict[42] = "This is NOT the meaning of life"
print dict[42]
```

This would output "This is NOT the meaning of life".

Functions

Python has a bunch of built-in functions, and it also comes with a whole list of modules and classes that can be used to construct your programs. In most cases, you will start by building functions, and those functions may, or may not, be combined into modules at some point. We'll take it a step at a time.

For RPG programmers, at least the more "modern" ones (whoever they are), monolithic code is an anathema. It's hard to read, hard to debug, and hard to share. And if you do decide to share or copy it, then if you tweak the "mother" of the others, you need to update the others as well. Most RPG and COBOL programmers I know abandoned that technique about the time that Prince changed his name to ... well, whatever it was changed to. What replaced the monolithic coding style? Well, subroutines were the first step, and then subprocedures, and then those were gathered into service programs, which made for nice, neat bundles of goodness in the ILE world. Leveraging those service programs across multiple applications made for nice, easy-to-maintain code. I am not going to make you relive that process; we'll just start at the service program equivalent: functions with modules.

Modules are just groups of functions gathered into a source file that can be included in other source files. There isn't much magic to modules; you just need to "import" them when you need the functions within them, kind of like using a BNDDIR in your H-specs to reference a procedure in a service module.

Functions come in all shapes and sizes. Functions begin with a def and finish with a return (in most cases). Between the def and return would be 1) a function name followed by parentheses, 2) input parameters to go within the parentheses if needed, 3) a colon (:), 4) an optional string that describes what the function is (docstring), 5) a block of code, and 6) a return statement that could return a value to the caller or can just be left blank.

A prototype would be like this:

```
def myfunctionname( parameters ):
    "Function description (docstring)"
    a_bunch_of_code
    return [expression]
```

Let's continue the example by going back to some of the code above and "functionalizing" it. Remember that we tiptoed through the tuples like so:

```
languages = 'Python','Ruby','JavaScript',42, 77.5
print languages

print languages[2]
print languages[-2]

for x in languages: print x
```

We can create a function that would handle just that bit of code:

```
def tttt(languages) :
        "Tiptoeing through the tuples"
        print languages
        print languages[2]
        print languages[-2]
        for x in languages: print x
        return

# Create a tuple variable
mytuple = 'Python','Ruby','JavaScript',42, 77.5

# Run our code
tttt(mytuple)
```

The output is just the same as before:

```
('Python', 'Ruby', 'JavaScript', 42, 77.5)
JavaScript
42
Python
```

Continued

```
Ruby
JavaScript
42
77.5
```

I need to mention something that is unique to Python, and that is *indentation matters*. This will probably come back to you time and time again, since I often get it wrong myself. It doesn't matter if you indent using tabs or spaces; just be consistent and make sure your indentations are properly relative to each other. This is where a good text editor that can syntax-check your Python will be very helpful.

Modules

If you took the function and stuffed it inside a file called myMod.py, you could then use that function by issuing the following:

```
import myMod
# Create a tuple variable
mytuple = 'Python','Ruby','JavaScript',42, 77.5

# Run our code
myMod.tttt(mytuple)
```

You'd get the same output with the added advantage that you can use the tttt function in other programs with just one line of code: import myMod.

That is about all the complexity that a module has: it is a file containing one or more functions, and usually those functions are in the module because the functionality they bring to the party is broad-based. Outside of easing maintenance by locating similar functions in a single file, the utility of a module is that typically the functions they encapsulate can be used in multiple programs.

I didn't mention scope, but since the parameters are passed by reference, you need to remember that variables declared local to the function are private to that function. For example, suppose you have a function like this:

```
def sayit(phrase):
        "This demonstrates scope"
        print phrase
        phrase = "Inside the function "
        print phrase
        return

myphrase = "Outside the function"
sayit(myphrase)
print myphrase
```

Part of me expects that the phrase variable would be changed because it was changed inside the function. But I'd be disappointed. Here is what we get:

```
Outside the function
Inside the function
Outside the function
```

We get that result because the phrase variable declared inside the function is "local" to the function, even though it may be the same name as the parameter passed in.

When declared as above, the parameters are required. If we ran the same code as above but, instead of calling sayit(phrase), we forgot and called sayit(), we would see this:

```
    sayit()
TypeError: sayit() takes exactly 1 argument (0 given)
```

So, if you need three parameters, then you *have to* have three parameters passed to it, and they all need to be in the correct order that the function expects them in.

Another possible way to pass parameters would be to use keywords when the parameters are passed to the function. Suppose you had a function like this:

```
def printit(name, address):
      "Doesn't matter what order!"
      print "Name: ", name
      print "Address:", address
      return

myname = "Joe Zablotnik"
myaddress = "123 Main Street"

printit(name=myname, address=myaddress)
# Order doesn't matter
printit(address=myaddress, name=myname)
```

The output is:

```
Name:   Joe Zablotnik
Address: 123 Main Street
Name:   Joe Zablotnik
Address: 123 Main Street
```

Remove the keywords, and you'll get this:

```
Name:   Joe Zablotnik
Address: 123 Main Street
Name:   123 Main Street
Address: Joe Zablotnik
```

If you are not sure how many parameters you'll be passing, you can always allow any number of arguments to be passed in, like so:

```
def printit(*stuffin):
      "Number of parms in doesn't matter!"
      if(len(stuffin)>=1):
            print "Name: ", stuffin[0]
      if(len(stuffin)==2):
```
Continued

```
            print "Address:", stuffin[1]
        return

myname = "Joe Zablotnik"
myaddress = "123 Main Street"

printit(myname, myaddress)
# one or two, it doesn't matter to the function
printit(myaddress)
```

The function doesn't really care, but we need to at least figure out how many parms were passed in because we need to deal with them in the code. That means we evaluate how many were passed in and handle them individually. Note also that the passed parameters are tuples.

Perhaps a clearer way to handle a variable number of variables would be to use keyword variables so we know what we are looking for, and when we find it, we use it, like this:

```
def printit(**stuffin):
        "Number of parms doesn't matter!"
        if 'name' in stuffin:
            print "Name: ", stuffin['name']
        if 'address' in stuffin:
            print "Address:", stuffin['address']

        return

myname = "Joe Zablotnik"
myaddress = "123 Main Street"

printit(name = myname, address = myaddress)
# one or two, it doesn't matter to the function
printit(address = myaddress)
```

So far, so good, and no convolutions like "blocks" in Ruby.

But if we stray into the realm of anonymous functions in Python, then things get a little "out there." Anonymous functions are relatively unknown to IBM i programmers unless they are JavaScript developers, Ruby developers, or Java developers using Java 8. Basically, an anonymous function allows you to declare a function without needing a def and a return. In Python, they are known as lambda functions (JavaScript and Ruby have them as well). They sound a bit freakish, and in some respects they are, but they can be pretty useful in some situations. The best example I could assemble looks like this (and now for something completely different):

```
def increment_it (n): return lambda x: x + n

fii = increment_it(2)
gii = increment_it(6)

print fii(42), gii(42)

print increment_it(22)(33)
```

Let's take it a step at a time.

In the example above, we are declaring a "regular" function (increment_it), but we return the value to a lambda, along with a parameter, and the lambda function then returns a value. increment_it as a function takes a single value and returns. But that return then passes it to a lambda function, which has one parameter that takes the return value and adds whatever was passed to it to the value passed to increment_it. So that is a killer first line. The second and third lines could appear equally cryptic, but remember that variables in Python are dynamic and can hold any object, and in this case fii and gii are lambda functions themselves that will be initialized with the increments of 2 and 6, respectively. Let me say that again: fii and gii are variables holding lambda functions with slightly different values for increment_it. The very last line shows how the whole thing is invoked, passing 22 as the increment to increment_it, and 33 will be passed to the lambda function. Here are the results:

```
44 48
55
```

Pretty nice. Lambda become helpful in just these kinds of situations where an output from a named function needs to be further processed without the overhead of writing a traditional function. You probably won't be writing a lambda right out of the blocks, but you are bound to run into them at some point. Might as well familiarize you with them now rather than have you run out of the room screaming hysterically later.

Classes in Python

Before we move on to a more complete code example, we have to embrace the object-oriented nature of Python by reviewing classes. As mentioned in other chapters of this book, a class is really a template of how an object should look and act. It defines the object's properties, data, and functions and provides a method for initializing and creating objects based on the class.

A simple example is this:

```python
class Talker:
    'The talker class'
    talkerCount = 0

    def __init__(self, greeting):
        self.greeting=greeting
        Talker.talkerCount+=1

    def speak_klingon(self):
        print "nuqneH"
        return

    def speak(self):
        print self.greeting
        return

talker1 = Talker("Hola")
talker2 = Talker("Bonjour")

talker1.speak_klingon()
```

Continued

```
talker2.speak_klingon()

talker1.speak()
talker2.speak()

print Talker.talkerCount
```

This is simple and contrived, but it demonstrates a few things. First, you can have an initialization routine that takes the initial value and stores it in an instance variable in the object when created. Second, you have a class variable that will be shared across all instances of the class (that is the Talker.talkerCount as opposed to using something like self.talkerCount). Third, Klingon is the universal language spoken by all Talkers.

The output would be:

```
nuqneH
nuqneH
Hola
Bonjour
2
```

If you included a module for speaking Klingon, klingon.py, you could just include the module in your Talker class so that all talkers would speak Klingon. Take a look.

Our klingon.py has this:

```
def speak_klingon():
        print "nuqneH"
        return
```

And our Talker class now looks like this:

```
class Talker:
        import klingon
```
Continued

```
'The talker class'
talkerCount = 0

def __init__(self, greeting):
        self.greeting=greeting
        Talker.talkerCount+=1

def speak(self):
        print self.greeting
        return
```

Invoke the code:

```
talker1 = Talker("Hola")
talker2 = Talker("Bonjour")

talker1.klingon.speak_klingon()
talker2.klingon.speak_klingon()

talker1.speak()
talker2.speak()

print Talker.talkerCount
```

The output:

```
nuqneH
nuqneH
Hola
Bonjour
2
```

File Access in Python

How about a simple example with a little more oomph and less mystery? File access is something you'll probably be doing on a regular basis, and Python has no problems with file access. Let's build a file and read through it. Here is the whole tamale:

```
import csv

# write inventory data as comma-separated values
writer = csv.writer(open('inventory.csv', 'wb', buffering=0))
writer.writerows([
    ('WIG', 'Colorful widgets', 'Blue', 300, 1.99),
    ('FOOBARS', 'Tasty Foo bars', 'Chocolate', 125, 1.75),
    ('GAG', 'Various Gadgets', 'N/A', 500, 2.29),
    ('DOODADS','Marvelous doodads','Green',1000,19.99),
    ('THINGAMABOBS','What ARE these things?','Unknown',750,4.95)
])

# read inventory data, print status messages
inventory = csv.reader(open('inventory.csv', 'rb'))
status_labels = {-1: 'low', 0: 'adequate', 1: 'over stocked'}
for stock_ID, title, description, qty, price in inventory:
    status = status_labels[cmp(int(qty), 500)]
    print '%s is %s (%s)' % (title, status, qty)
```

Don't ya just love it? With very little code, you can get a boatload of work done.

Most of the magic is in that first line: import csv. That module provides quite a bit of functionality, and we get all of it on that one line. The first line is a comment (the # sign denotes comments). The second line may look a little foreign to someone who hasn't spent time in the object-oriented world, but there is real beauty in the second line. We have a variable that we are calling writer (good name, since it will be writing our data), and we assign that variable the result of a call to the writer function in the csv module. That writer takes an object returned from the open function, and the open function, which is a built-in function in Python, so it isn't qualified by a csv, takes a filename, a mode string, which identifies how the file should be created and used, and a third optional parameter that determines how the file I/O will be buffered. Open will return a handle to the file, which the writer object will reference to write to the file. I say "write" because the string 'wb' that was passed to open means that the file will be created if it doesn't exist; it will be open for writing, and it will contain binary data 'b'. We won't deep dive into file I/O, but there are plenty of options and methods at your disposal.

So, out of the wonderful second line of code, we get an object called writer (we could have called it anything). That object has functions that can be used to write to the file. The function we leverage immediately is writerows. Now, we could have used writerow (singular) and written the rows one at a time, but writerows allows us to push it all in in "one swell foop." Note that the parameter passed in is a sequence (array) of tuple objects. Yeah, you know this stuff!

Reading the file is just as easy. Again, the csv module has a reader function that returns a reader object we called inventory. The csv.reader function is passed a file object, which is returned from the built-in file open function that is passed the filename and the "mode," which is the string 'rb', which means the file is opened read-only for binary data.

The interesting part here is the status_labels variable, which has a dictionary object in it with three name-value pairs. Jump down a couple of lines to where the variable is actually used. You'll see that the status variable is populated by *three* functions rather tersely combined on the line. The cmp function compares two values and returns one of three results: It returns -1 if the left comparator is less than the right; it returns 0 if they are equal; and it returns 1 if the left comparator is greater than the right. We cast the qty parameter to an int so that the comparison is performed "apples to apples" (remember that our variables can be dynamically typed). Our comparison is to the integer 500, so our quantities in each inventory record are compared to 500 each time. The cool part is that the return value (-1, 0, or 1) is then used to retrieve a value from our status_labels dictionary—for example, status_labels[ ]. And *that* value is used as the value for the status variable. Nice!

System Access

In every chapter of this book, we have covered access to the system—the immediate system (PASE) and the IBM i system. Python is no slouch when it comes to capabilities. So we'll do "ice cream before spinach" and take a look at PASE access first. It is probably better thought of as "host" system access since calling (shelling) out to the system can be done in LUW as well as PASE.

In Python, here is how we begin the "Journey to the Center of the i": We use subprocess ... call to get there.

```
from subprocess import call
call(["ls", "/home/pete","-l"])
```

Basically, the script spawns a new process, executes the command, and then returns the output. Nothing fancy here. It is very similar to many other scripting languages. Where things get interesting is when you access IBM i resources. We can pretty much get to whatever we want on IBM i by using the XMLSERVICE library. Fortunately, Python also has a wrapper module in the iToolkit for Python. Let's take a look at this particular implementation of the Python client of XMLSERVICE.

DB2 Access

Again, we are fortunate to have the pioneers of open source doing all the heavy lifting for us on IBM i. There is already a Python module called ibm_db that handles all the I/O to DB2 on i and back again. All we need to do is use it.

Just an aside on getting the functionality. I went the PTF route in order to get the ibm_db and the iToolkit installed for Python. I also chose to install it for Python 3. I hate to give you links to the site because they get outdated so quickly, but I pulled the instructions from the IBM developerWorks site, which used pip3 to install the wheel (.whl) file. It seems that is the currently supported method. So plan on installing the correct PTF for your level of the operating system as well as installing using pip3. That sounds redundant, but it is not. pip3 installs from the IFS, but there isn't anything there unless you install the PTF first! So find the PTF, install the PTF, and then install the .whl using pip3. That worked for me.

Once you have the ibm_db module installed, you can use it. Let's look at an example in Python 3. (How do you know it is Python 3? The print() statements.)

```
import ibm_db
conn = ibm_db.connect("*LOCAL","myuserid","mypassword")
sql = "select * from employee.employee"
result_set = ibm_db.exec_immediate(conn,sql)
print("opening connection")
```
Continued

```
if conn:
        dictionary = ibm_db.fetch_both(result_set)
        while dictionary != False:
            print("Row is : ",dictionary["EMPID"] + " " +
            dictionary[1] + " " +dictionary[2])
            dictionary = ibm_db.fetch_both(result_set)

print("closing connection")
ibm_db.close(conn)
```

Note that in the dictionary that is returned, I can reference the columns by name or by ordinal position (dictionary["EMPID"] or dictionary[1....]). Plenty of I/O methods are available, so we are looking at only one here. But we used the "generic" ibm_db.exec_ immediate, which we could use for *any* SQL statements: SELECT, INSERT, DELETE, and so on. And, of course, there are methods that will allow us to bind parameters and execute prepared statements. The whole panoply of SQL goodness is available to you here. I encourage you to experiment (with a test database, of course).

Accessing RPG

Once again, we have "one call, that's all" for calling RPG from OSS, and that is: XMLSERVICE! Of course, you know this stuff! You'll need to make sure that the toolkit is properly installed using the same procedure as with the ibm_db module. But once you have the toolkit installed, there is just one thing to remember: require toolkit! Here is an example (similar to the others if you have read the other chapters):

```
from itoolkit.lib.ilibcall import *
itransport = iLibCall()
from itoolkit import *
# XMLSERVICE/ZZCALL:
#      D  INCHARA      S            1a
#      D  INCHARB      S            1a
#      D  INDEC1       S            7p 4
#      D  INDEC2       S            12p 2
```

Continued

```
#     D  INDS1              DS
#     D  DSCHARA                    1a
#     D  DSCHARB                    1a
#     D  DSDEC1                     7p 4
#     D  DSDEC2                     12p 2
#        *+++++++++++++++++++++++++++++++++++++++++++++++++++++++++++++++++
#        * main(): Control flow
#        *+++++++++++++++++++++++++++++++++++++++++++++++++++++++++++++++++
#     C     *Entry     PLIST
#     C                PARM                      INCHARA
#     C                PARM                      INCHARB
#     C                PARM                      INDEC1
#     C                PARM                      INDEC2
#     C                PARM                      INDS1
itool = iToolKit()
itool.add(iCmd('chglibl', 'CHGLIBL LIBL(XMLSERVICE)'))
itool.add(
 iPgm('zzcall','ZZCALL')
 .addParm(iData('INCHARA','1a','a'))
 .addParm(iData('INCHARB','1a','b'))
 .addParm(iData('INDEC1','7p4','32.1234'))
 .addParm(iData('INDEC2','12p2','33.33'))
 .addParm(
  iDS('INDS1')
  .addData(iData('DSCHARA','1a','a'))
  .addData(iData('DSCHARB','1a','b'))
  .addData(iData('DSDEC1','7p4','32.1234'))
  .addData(iData('DSDEC2','12p2','33.33'))
  )
 )

# xmlservice
itool.call(itransport)
```
Continued

```
# output
chglibl = itool.dict_out('chglibl')
if 'success' in chglibl:
  print (chglibl['success'])
else:
  print (chglibl['error'])
  exit()

zzcall = itool.dict_out('zzcall')
if 'success' in zzcall:
  print (zzcall['success'])
  print ("     INCHARA      : " + zzcall['INCHARA'])
  print ("     INCHARB      : " + zzcall['INCHARB'])
  print ("     INDEC1       : " + zzcall['INDEC1'])
  print ("     INDEC2       : " + zzcall['INDEC2'])
  print ("     INDS1.DSCHARA: " + zzcall['INDS1']['DSCHARA'])
  print ("     INDS1.DSCHARB: " + zzcall['INDS1']['DSCHARB'])
  print ("     INDS1.DSDEC1 : " + zzcall['INDS1']['DSDEC1'])
  print ("     INDS1.DSDEC2 : " + zzcall['INDS1']['DSDEC2'])
else:
  print (zzcall['error'])
  exit()
```

TMI! Let's unpack it because there is a bunch of scripting that adds to the verbosity when the actual *action* in the example is pretty simple. Import commands. We have two. The first pulls in the iLibCall method from the package itoolkit.lib.ilibcall. We then assign iLibCall to a variable (object) called itransport. iLibCall will use the XMLSERVICE library to make the direct call using the current connection (in my case, made using a shell in SSH). We can also use a DB2 stored procedure or a REST call using HTTP if we need to call into a remote system. The second import pulls in all methods from the itoolkit package. It isn't redundant because we won't get every method from *every* package with from itoolkit import *. We only get the methods and objects from the package. Import pulls in what we need from the itoolkit module.

The endless comments are just to show you the code that will be executed by the call. It will give you the program structure so you will know how to structure your own program call. It is *just* comments. Don't sweat the verbosity, OK?

Next, we create an itool object that contains most of the code to do the heavy lifting for us. Once we have that object, we immediately use it to add a command (an iCmd object cleverly called chglibl) to add XMLSERVICE to the library list. Then we add an iPgm object called zzcall to the itool object. The definition of that iPgm object has multiple parameters called iData objects that define the single-variable parameters and parameters called iDS objects that are data structures. But rather than adding parameters to the iDS object, you add data objects to the data structure. Logical, right?

Once you define the objects, adding them to your itool object, then you make your call using whatever transport you defined (direct, DB2, or REST). All the magic happens there. Now you just have to query the itool object to see if your call was successful. We actually had two things that ran: The CHGLIBL command, and the call to the ZZCALL program in XMLSERVICE.

Now we retrieve the results, storing the results in a dictionary (hash). We know the command was successful if the "success" key is in the dictionary. If we didn't find "success," then an "error" key would be available, and we could examine that value to see what went wrong. The same routine applies for our call to ZZCALL (why do I think of bearded guys when I see ZZCALL?). We check to see if our dictionary contains a "success" key, and if so, we retrieve the value, which is the name of the program we called, and then we walk the rest of the dictionary to retrieve the values associated with each parameter. Our print statements dutifully print out the contents of each parameter returned. Lather, rinse, and repeat with your stuff. It is tedious but eminently functional. No pain, no gain.

Feel the Power

What I have been trying to demonstrate in this chapter is the strength of Python: its terseness without being mystifying and its utility and flexibility. For IBM i folks, that should be familiar territory. Our command-line commands are very terse yet, arguably, about as descriptive as a three-letter command can be. The object-oriented nature of Python also appeals to the Java programmer in me. Yes, I see the same kind of power in JavaScript and PHP and Ruby, but it nicely comes together in Python.

10

Node.js on IBM i

This will be the first "bait and switch" chapter (maybe not). You know, like that $50 mobile phone plan that gives you "unlimited" calling, data, and texting, as long as you are on a public Wi-Fi? Doh! Well, in this case, the "bait" was dangling "Node.js" in front of you, and the switch is jumping right into ... JavaScript. The reason for the switch is that there is no "Node.js" language. Here is the definition of Node.js from Wikipedia:

"In software development, Node.js is an open-source, cross-platform runtime environment for developing server-side applications. Although Node.js is not a JavaScript framework, many of its basic modules are written in JavaScript, and developers can write new modules in JavaScript. The runtime environment interprets JavaScript using Google's V8 JavaScript engine."

So, let's unpack that. Open source: check! Cross-platform: Yep! Otherwise we'd be talking about ILE RPG as the language. And then the mouthful: "runtime environment for developing server-side applications."

So the first thing to pay attention to is the mention of "server." Node.js is a server just like your IBM i is an application server. If you happen to use Tomcat or PHP on your IBM i, those are application servers as well. It gets to be a little like those Russian matryoshka dolls that are nested inside of each other: you have an IBM i (server) running Node .js (server), which may be running the plug-in called http-server (server). The operative words to pay attention to are "server" and "Web" and "JavaScript." I personally think that is where the great utility comes into play. In Node.js, you have a server platform that can serve Web content, and it is a server that uses JavaScript as the base language. As a Web developer, you'll be bumping into JavaScript basically everywhere, so being able to leverage a language like JavaScript in your "regular" development is a plus in my opinion.

So because Node.js is a server that runs JavaScript, we are going to 1) go through the basics of the JavaScript language and 2) talk about "plugging in" modules in Node.js and how to maintain and write modules for Node.js. Then once we have background on the language, we will walk through our "usual" routine of accessing "local" system commands (PASE in our case), accessing database resources in DB2 for IBM i land, accessing the IBM i command line, and finally making calls to the big wide world of RPG!

Jiving with JavaScript

JavaScript in the Web world has had, and some say still has, a checkered past. Reviled in the late 1990s because of the ease with which it could be exploited for malicious purposes on the Web, it is now, remarkably, the core language for a Web server (Node.js!). The "exploit" side of things is still a risk, primarily in the browser, but the ease with which you can grasp the basics of the language, the plethora of examples and tutorials that exist for free on the Web, and the current romance that the bleeding-edge Web developers have with Node.js make it a great choice for developers looking to add some "dev cred" to their resumes.

JavaScript's most well-known characteristics are that it is a high-level language (which makes it almost self-documenting), is untyped (which we will talk about), interpreted (which is changing), and is object-oriented (where the power resides!). It is easy to learn, requires no real IDE to use in development (a text editor is enough), and can be run from an HTML form in almost any browser.

Although scripting languages have been around for ages (BASIC and BasicScript come to mind), the rise of using a scripting language in a Web environment coincided with the rise of the Web. For those who are old enough to remember those early days, the 800-pound gorilla of browsers was from Netscape, and those folks developed the first versions of what we call JavaScript today. Microsoft developed VBScript and JScript for the Internet Explorer browser, but Netscape submitted the specification of JavaScript to ECMA, which established an ECMAScript (ES) standard that lives on today. So as of this writing, ES6 is the nascent version now being adopted, ES7 has been released (aka ES 2016), and ES 2017 is in the pipeline. In 2016, the naming and versioning plan changed, and the plan now is to release versions more quickly, perhaps annually, so I wonder, what is the version you will use in 2025?

If you want to "run" a JavaScript script, you have a few choices. A browser can be used if you embed the JavaScript in an HTML form and then use the debugging or developer tools to monitor output. Of course, an easy solution is to run Node.js. For the more adventuresome, you can compile or find a binary for the Google V8 engine and run it in the command window or terminal. For the examples we'll be running, I am using the Sublime Text text editor, which uses my installed version of Node.js for the runtime environment. There are also other scripting shells available that you can find on the Internet. A scripting shell is also known as a REPL: Read, Evaluate, Print, Loop. In any case, I highly recommend finding something to run the examples with. Trial and error is a great teacher.

JavaScript is both an object-oriented (OO) and a procedural language. You can structure your code however you want (similar to PHP). So, the good news for an RPG programmer is that you don't have to fully embrace OO techniques in order to make use of the language. But, we are going to go there anyway because it's cool and productive, and even more so, most code you will come across in the Node.js world will be OO. So put on your "big kid" pants, and let's start!

Take a look at this example:

```
var name1 = "Joe Zablotnik";
var age1 = 40;
var address1 = "123 main street";

var name2 = "Pikofp Andropoff";
var age2 = 30;
var address2 = "444 Gorby street";
```

Continued

```
console.log(name1 + ":");
console.log(name1 + " age is " + age1);
console.log("and " + name1 + " lives at " + address1);
console.log("");
console.log(name2 +":");
console.log(name2 + " age is " + age2);
console.log("and " + name1 + "lives at " + address2);
```

The output would be:

```
Joe Zablotnik:
Joe Zablotnik age is 40
and Joe Zablotnik lives at 123 main street

Pikofp Andropoff:
Pikofp Andropoff age is 30
and Pikofp Andropoff lives at 444 Gorby street
```

If you wanted to retrieve and print 100 names and addresses in this way, it would be pretty tedious.

Take a look at this alternative:

```
var person1 = new Object;
var person2 = {};  // another way of declaring an object

person1.name = "Joe Zablotnik";
person1.age = 40;
person1.address = "123 main street";

person2.name = "Pikofp Andropoff";
person2.age = 30;
person2.address = "444 Gorby street";
```
Continued

```
function spillthebeans(p){
        console.log(p.name+ ":");
        console.log(p.name + " age is " + p.age);
        console.log("and " + p.name + " lives at " + p.address);
        console.log("");
}

spillthebeans(person1);
spillthebeans(person2);
```

You say to yourself, "Pete is a genius! He went from 15 lines of code to 21. He must be paid by the line!" Well, that isn't true, but you still might be scratching your head about how the alternative presented here is "better." The "better" part is revealed as the number of "persons" increases. The function that outputs the information will always stay at six lines while in the original, more procedural approach you will add the four lines of code to output for each new "person" added. Thinking in OO terms, as was described in chapter 5, is what is needed here. The point is to attempt to encapsulate the object concept into your designs.

So, with that brief introduction to the rationale behind OO design, let's back up a bit and deal with some basic programming concepts in JavaScript: variables (dynamic typing), scope, objects and classes, arrays and hashes, and functions. The other nuts and bolts of programming in JavaScript will be well known to any experienced programmer, so we won't be jumping in too deeply on either the well-known concepts or the arcana of the language.

JavaScript is a dynamically typed language, so you could do something like this:

```
var meaningoflife = "He who dies with the most toys wins";
console.log(meaningoflife);

meaningoflife = 42;
console.log(meaningoflife);
```

Continued

```
function mylife(){
stuff = 5;
while(stuff>=0){
console.log("Keep using stuff until it is all gone. Stuff is now "
+stuff);
stuff--;
}
console.log("My stuff is all gone!");
}

meaningoflife = mylife;

meaningoflife();
```

The output would be:

```
He who dies with the most toys wins
42
Keep using stuff until it is all gone. Stuff is now 5
Keep using stuff until it is all gone. Stuff is now 4
Keep using stuff until it is all gone. Stuff is now 3
Keep using stuff until it is all gone. Stuff is now 2
Keep using stuff until it is all gone. Stuff is now 1
Keep using stuff until it is all gone. Stuff is now 0
My stuff is all gone!
```

The thing that is most notable here is that we see a declared variable assigned not only to different values but different types. JavaScript won't complain about it. I don't recommend that you take such a cavalier attitude to variable type assignment. I note it because since an error is not thrown when such reassignment takes place, you could end up stomping on a variable, which may come back to haunt you. Like this:

```
var meaningoflife = 42;
console.log(parseInt(meaningoflife) );
meaningoflife = "He who dies with the most toys wins";
console.log(parseInt(meaningoflife) );
```

Rarely would you do such a quick reassignment of a variable type, but imagine if you defined a variable called account and assigned it a string account number, but later on in your code you began to use the same variable as an account balance. JavaScript wouldn't complain, but your users would. It would also be devilishly difficult to debug (take my word for it!). So I *do* see variable names like str_name and int_balance where the type is part of the variable name. It can be useful.

Scope plays into the whole untyped variable scenario as well. Take this example, for instance:

```
var x = 42;

function addandoutput(inx){

        x="the number is ";
        y = x + inx;
        console.log(y);

}

console.log(x);

addandoutput(x);

console.log(x);
```

The output will be:

```
42
the number is 42
the number is
```

You start with a variable that has a value of 42. You inadvertently assign it to a string, so you end up with a string, stomping on the original value. That is why you want to do two things on a regular basis: 1) use a variable name that indicates its type (if possible) and 2) *always* use "var" when defining the variable for the *first* time. If something weird is happening in your code that seems drop-dead simple, check for scope issues as well. We could rewrite the code above like so:

```
var x = 42;

function addandoutput(inx){
        var x="the number is ";
        var y = x + inx;
        console.log(y);

}

console.log(x);

addandoutput(x);

console.log(x);
```

The output will be:

```
42
the number is 42
42
```

That's better!

So what kind of dynamic data types are most common? I'd say the following are the ones you are most likely to encounter:

- var int_length = 42; // Number
- var str_number = "Forty two"; // String
- var ary_lang = ["RPG", "Ruby", "Python"]; // Array (
- var person = {firstName:"John", lastName:"Doe"}; // Object (more about this syntax [JSON] later)
- var bool_true_false = true; // boolean true/false

There are also a couple of constants that you will get familiar with, even though you may not fully understand them at first:

- undefined—The variable has no type and no value. Most variables are in this state until assigned a value.

- null—No value and type is object. A null value is always an object. For example:

```
var x = 42;
 console.log( typeof x);  // ==> number
x = null;
 console.log( typeof x);  // ==> object
```

JavaScript also has plenty of built-in functions. typeof is one built-in function that retrieves the type of variable you are dealing with. There are built-in math methods you can access from the Math object, like Math.random(), Math.min(), Math.max(), and many more. There are String methods like substring(), indexOf(), slice(), and a host of others. All of this is well documented on the Web. Google is my programming "pair" when I am in development mode.

There are a few things beyond the basics of variable types and methods that you'll need to wrap your head around. These are pretty common to most OO languages. As I had reviewed in chapter 5, the cool thing about objects in the OO world is that they contain data and methods. They are like mini-programs in themselves, and leveraging the concepts of inheritance and polymorphism can really improve your productivity. Just like modular programming and the concept of code reuse in Don't Repeat Yourself (DRY) development (covered in chapter 7), leveraging OO concepts can let you focus on writing new code and new routines while leveraging your prior work.

Classes and Objects

Let's go back to the very first example that demonstrated the advantage of using less procedural and more OO techniques. Remember building that "person" object?

```
var person1 = new Object;
```

Continued

```
person1.name = "Joe Zablotnik";
person1.age = 40;
person1.address = "123 main street";
```

Turns out that is a very ES5 way of doing things. If you are using the latest version of Node.js and using a Web browser that actually works, like Chrome or Firefox, you can use some of the "class" concepts I talked about in chapter 5. Imagine building a Person class that defines a constructor to create a person object as well as a method to output the person information. That class might look like this:

```
'use strict';

class Person {
constructor(fName, age, address) {
// Properties
this.fullName = fName;
this.age = age;
this.address = address;
}
// Methods
talkAboutMe() {
        return 'My name is ${this.fullName} I am a ${this.age}-yr. old
programmer that lives on ${this.address}';
}
}
```

Again, this is a wee bit more code than before, but the goal here is that in the long term we'll make up for slightly longer code that defines the class with less code to implement the class. What is really nice about this is the constructor and the method. It is all self-contained, so when we build a person we already have an object that can talk about itself (maybe the class should be "Politician"). So this is how we would then construct one of these persons and get it to talk:

```
var me = new Person("Pete Helgren", "33", "19001 Huebner road");

console.log(me.talkAboutMe());
```

Output:

```
My name is Pete Helgren I am a 33-yr. old programmer that lives on
19001 Huebner road
```

(Apparently this person also lies about their age ... they *are* a politician!)

The ES5 aficionado will say "I can do that with an object by passing parameters to a function to set all the properties as well." Well, yeah, that is the way most folks used to do it, but now we can *also* use inheritance with the "extend" keyword, so that if we have a class that we want to extend with another class's function, we can do that!

Let's say this Person class extends the Employee class. The Employee class has the following:

```
class Employee {
        constructor(hireDate, monthlyPay) {
        this.hireDate = hireDate;
        this.monthlyPay = monthlyPay;
        }
getMonthlySalary() {
        return 'Killer!  I make ${this.monthlySalary} each month.'
        }
}
```

Note that the Employee class has a constructor as well, so we'll need to accommodate that when we construct the Person class that extends Employee. So our complete class would look like this:

```
'use strict';

class Employee {
      constructor(hireDate, monthlyPay) {
      this.hireDate = hireDate;
      this.monthlyPay = monthlyPay;
      }
getMonthlySalary() {
      return 'Killer! I make ${this.monthlySalary} each month.'
      }
}

class Person extends Employee{
constructor(fName, age , address, hireDate, monthlySalary) {
      // Call the contructor for Employee
      super(hireDate, monthlySalary);
// Person Properties
this.fullName = fName;
this.age = age;
this.address = address;
}
// Methods
talkAboutMe() {
      return 'My name is ${this.fullName} I am a ${this.age}-yr. old
programmer that lives on ${this.address}';
}
}

var me = new Person("Pete Helgren", "33", "19001 Huebner road",
"09/01/2012", 1.99);

console.log(me.talkAboutMe());
console.log(me.getMonthlySalary());
```

Then the output would be:

```
My name is Pete Helgren I am a 33-yr. old programmer that lives on
19001 Huebner road
Killer!  I make 1.99 each month.
```

How sweet is that? By just extending the class with another class, I inherit the data storage and the methods of that class. Hopefully, you are beginning to get the big picture here. In many cases, we build programs that use and reuse code, not only within the same program but across programs as well. By creating classes, we can reuse common functions just by extending the class with another class. Very often, you will develop quite a few utility programs that handle I/O, or validation or, in the cases of security, encoding/decoding and verifying information. Classes allow us to reuse use our commonly used stuff.

Arrays and Hashes

We have already traveled a little way down this path. We have walked through basic variable types, and an array was mentioned as a type. Hashes are really just objects that have name/value pairs (key/value pairs) that on the face of it, don't have much utility. But as we stray into the Web world and use JSON as a way of representing/moving data, the whole name/value pairing becomes pretty powerful.

Let's first take a look at arrays because I think they will be pretty familiar to RPG programmers and programmers in general. In JavaScript we can construct an array in one of a couple of ways:

```
var myarray = [42, 'life', 1984, 1492, 'zebra'];
```

Like most things in JavaScript, we are dealing with dynamically typed data, so we can have any kind of stuff stuffed into an array. To retrieve data from an array, you just reference the cell the data is stored in:

```
console.log(myarray[2]);
```

which would return 1984.

We could also create an array like this:

```
var mynewarray = new Array(42, 'life', 1984, 1492, 'zebra');
console.log(mynewarray[3]);
```

which would return 1492.

The new Array() syntax should ring a few bells, and at least one light bulb should go on. You should be thinking to yourself, "Wait a minute, if it has a constructor, it must be an object!" Right you are! So what else does an array object have that we might make use of? Take a look at the following example:

```
fLen = myarray.length;
for (i = 0; i < fLen; i++) {
    console.log("Item at " + i + " is " + myarray[i] );
}
```

Using the data from above, the output would be:

```
Item at 0 is 42
Item at 1 is life
Item at 2 is 1984
Item at 3 is 1492
Item at 4 is zebra
```

So the array will have a length object that is a count of the items in the array. We can also "push" things onto the array and "pop" things off:

myarray.pop(); // removes the last element

myarray.push('antelope'); // adds 'antelope' to the end of the array

Then iterate through them again:

```
Item at 0 is 42
Item at 1 is life
Item at 2 is 1984
Item at 3 is 1492
Item at 4 is antelope
```

Hashes have a similar "feel," but because they are basically arrays without the index, you can access the contents differently. Rather than referencing their position in the stack, you reference the location by the "name" or "key" of the name/value pair. So let's recreate the array as a hash making up keys to reference each value.

One way we could create our hash is like so:

```
var myhash = {'mol':42, 'love':'life', 'bb':1984, 'columbus':1492,
'animal':'zebra'};
```

And if we wanted to get a single value, we could reference its location using the name/key:

```
console.log(myhash['bb']); // returns 1984
```

We can get an array of keys in the hash/object by using the Object.keys method. It will return the following for the myhash object:

```
console.log(Object.keys(myhash));
[ 'mol', 'love', 'bb', 'columbus', 'animal' ]
```

OK. Cool enough, but what use is it? In the command-line environment, iterating through key/value pairs may not be all that helpful. Certainly it has some utility, but how often will I be constructing and iterating though objects at the command line? Probably not very often. But hook this up to something with large amounts of I/O, like a database or a Web page, or both, and suddenly sorting through arrays of data or extracting data from objects becomes pretty important. Put the data and program that iterates through in on two different servers, and, man, most of your time could be spent parsing and sorting through data. That is where the concept of a "hash" becomes very useful! I briefly mentioned JSON, and it has become the "lingua franca" of the data-exchange world. The reason that the JSON format is so useful is ... well, let me show you an example, and you can tell me.

Let's say we have an array of objects, and each of those objects represents a person. Take a look at this:

```
var myjsondata = [
{"firstname": "John","lastname": "Doe","age": 50,"eyecolor": "blue"},
{"firstname": "Pete","lastname": "Helgren","age": 56,"eyecolor":
"green"},
{"firstname": "Bubba","lastname": "Gump","age": 32,"eyecolor": "brown"},
{"firstname": "Frank","lastname": "Zappa","age": 56,"eyecolor": "gray"},
{"firstname": "Ima","lastname": "Minion","age": 18,"eyecolor": "black"},
{"firstname": "Ima","lastname": "Hacker","age": 15,"eyecolor":
"crossed"}
]
```

Classic JSON format! The *only* difference here is that with JSON all of the keys/names are in double quotes. That's it! The utility comes in that as we evaluate each "record" in the array. Each array element contains an object {}. Those objects all have the same properties: firstname,lastname, age, and eyecolor. They don't *have* to have the same properties—this looks more like an array of database records, but in any case, we can walk through the array and interrogate each object in the array pretty simply:

```
var myjsondata = [
{"firstname": "John","lastname": "Doe","age": 50,"eyecolor": "blue"},
{"firstname": "Pete","lastname": "Helgren","age": 56,"eyecolor":
"green"},
{"firstname": "Bubba","lastname": "Gump","age": 32,"eyecolor": "brown"},
{"firstname": "Frank","lastname": "Zappa","age": 56,"eyecolor": "gray"},
{"firstname": "Ima","lastname": "Minion","age": 18,"eyecolor": "black"},
```
Continued

```
{"firstname": "Ima","lastname": "Hacker","age": 15,"eyecolor":
"crossed"}
];

fLen = myjsondata.length;

for (i = 0; i < fLen; i++) {
        // we know, just by looking at the data, that we have object
        // properties to iterate through as well
        // so get the object and walk the properties
        var myhash = myjsondata[i];
        Object.keys(myhash).forEach(function (key) {
    var value = myhash[key];
    // iteration code
    console.log("Item " + i + " with " + key + " is " +value);
        });
}
```

The output looks like this:

```
Item 0 with firstname is John
Item 0 with lastname is Doe
Item 0 with age is 50
Item 0 with eyecolor is blue
Item 1 with firstname is Pete
Item 1 with lastname is Helgren
Item 1 with age is 56
Item 1 with eyecolor is green
Item 2 with firstname is Bubba
Item 2 with lastname is Gump
Item 2 with age is 32
Item 2 with eyecolor is brown
Item 3 with firstname is Frank
Item 3 with lastname is Zappa
Item 3 with age is 56
Item 3 with eyecolor is gray
```

```
Item 4 with firstname is Ima
Item 4 with lastname is Minion
Item 4 with age is 18
Item 4 with eyecolor is black
Item 5 with firstname is Ima
Item 5 with lastname is Hacker
Item 5 with age is 15
Item 5 with eyecolor is crossed
```

Basically we iterated through the array and the properties of each object in the array. You'll find yourself doing this quite a bit when you are working with HTML—perhaps when you build a drop-down list of values, formatted as a select option, or when you create a report in HTML. We basically have five lines of code! Not bad (unless we are paid by the line).

Functions

We have been writing and using functions all along without much commentary, so it's time to back up and deal with them. You know what functions are, so I don't really need to explain *what* they are. You have been writing subroutines and subprocedures for years and, basically, those would be the equivalent of what a function is in JavaScript. Sometimes they are called *functions* when they stand alone, and sometimes they are called *methods* when encapsulated in a class or object. Basically it is a chunk of code you reference by a name and pass it parameters, except when you don't. Functions can be named in JavaScript or anonymous. Anonymous functions have no name and are usually assigned to a variable. You see anonymous functions quite a bit in asynchronous functions like ajax (xhr) calls because the asynchronous methods usually return data or pass a callback; in those cases, naming the function would be superfluous. Let's take a quick tour of functions in JavaScript and see what they can bring to the party.

At its simplest, a JavaScript named function will have a name, a function body, and probably a few statements to be run. A simple example would be:

```
function sayHello(pName){

        console.log("Hello "+pName);
```
Continued

```
        // In HTML this would pop up an alert box:
        //alert("Hello "+pName);

}
```

You could also assign a function to a variable. When you do that, you are actually creating an anonymous function and then assigning it to the variable.

```
var blarg = function(pName){ console.log("Hello " + pName) };
```

Then you could invoke it:

```
blarg("Pete");
```

It would output "Hello Pete".

We didn't talk about "hoisting" before because it is a little weird and is probably less obvious with variables. Hoisting is JavaScript's default behavior of moving variable (and function) declarations to the top of the script. You won't *see* them move; the JavaScript runtime will "hoist" those suckers to the top. So you might see something like this in a script:

```
x=1;
z=10;
var y = x + z;
1 = rocknroll(y);
```

And you'd be wondering where the heck those variables are declared. Where is the rocknroll function? Well, it could be *way* down in the script body. I tend to be a bit more tidy than that and naturally declare my stuff that will be global or used throughout a script at the top of the script, but that doesn't always happen. JavaScript "helps" you out by automagically moving declarations to the top. Beware the initialization weirdness that can happen! You might have code like this:

```
var x = 5; // Initialize x
console.log ( x + y);
var y = 7; // Initialize y
```

And the log statement displays "NaN" (not a number). What!? Both 5 and 7 are numbers, so why is the product of them *not* a number? It's because the *declaration* of *y* is hoisted. In reality, here is what JavaScript did to "help" you:

```
var x = 5;
var y;
console.log ( x + y);
y=7;
```

Isn't that helpful? That kind of stuff can drive you nuts. So, if you *think* you have all of your declarations correct and are seeing weird errors, take a careful look at what "hoisting" might have done to you.

So you can create functions and name them or assign them to variables. You can also have the function return some data as well, and you use a return statement to do that. We could write our sayHello function like this:

```
function sayHello(pName){
        return "Hello " + pname;
}

console.log(sayHello("Pete"));
```

We can create an object and put a function into it:

```
class Person {
constructor(fName, age , occupation, address) {
// Properties
                                                Continued
```

```
this.fullName = fName;
this.age = age;
this.address = address;
this.occupation = occupation;
}
// Methods
talkAboutMe() {
        return 'My name is ${this.fullName} I am a ${this.age}-yr. old
${occupation} that lives on ${this.address}';
}
}

// Create one

var me = new Person("Pete Helgren", "33", "Developer", "19001 Huebner
road");

console.log(me.talkAboutMe());
```

This is a pretty good overall demonstration of a function called from an object. Once we have created the Person, we can invoke the talkAboutMe method with dotted notation from the object. Nice.

Just a few more caveats. Occasionally you might forget to indicate that you *are* calling a function and simply call the function without the parentheses. Doing this will get you the function definition rather than the function. Every once in a while, you'll see a self-invoking function (illegal in three states!) that may look a little strange:

```
(function sayHola(){
        var pName = "Pete";
        console.log("Hola " + pName);
})();
```

Note the parentheses () at the end invoke the function directly. Again, this is a fairly rare use case, but it is something you may trip against, nonetheless. We will see an example of this as we visit Node.js.

Are we there yet? Can we get to know Node.js a little now? Yes, now would be a good time.

Node.js

Sure, the chapter was *supposed* to be on Node.js, but we have spent all of our time in JavaScript. You have to remember that Node.js is (as we mentioned at the beginning of the chapter) "an open-source, cross-platform runtime environment for developing server-side applications." Node.js is a server that is written in JavaScript with the V8 engine at its core, running modules that are, by and large, written in JavaScript. So a good grounding in JavaScript is necessary to wrap your head around the code. The really good news here is that there is much, *much* of the heavy lifting done for you because there is a plethora of modules that will do already what you want to do. So, we'll be leveraging a lot of the available modules in our examples because writing them from scratch would be a waste of time. We will spend some time talking about npm, the node package manager, and *then* we'll look at examples of how to implement our brilliant ideas in Node.js.

The node package manager was a necessary first step because it was quickly realized, as it was with Ruby/Rails, that integrating functional components from other sources would be a highly efficient way to build applications. The great thing about open source is that the community is always learning from the past, taking the best practices, properties, and attributes of other languages and projects and integrating them into the current languages and projects. Thus, when it came to creating a package manager for Node.js as it rapidly grew, the developers leveraged the things like wget, gem, rpm, PEAR, CPAN, and a host of others, no doubt. The concept of getting a package from a remote repository and installing it isn't new. *How* it is done is the key, and npm does it well.

There are a few caveats to using npm. Recently the interdependent nature of npm modules was exposed when a developer of a set of base modules, used practically everywhere, decided to yank his npm modules due to a dispute over naming conventions and trademark infringement. The removal of this module from the repository caused the other modules that depended on the module to not install (missing dependency!) and brought no end of woe to users of Node.js and npm for a few anxious days. The folks at npm restored the missing modules, but the problem has led to some changes on how the modules are managed and how they can be removed from the repository. In addition, modules are given a cursory vetting for security issues, coding practices, or malicious intent—so, as always, *caveat emptor*, even if it is free.

npm is included with Node.js, so there isn't anything you need to install to use it. You just run npm install <package name>. There are a couple of different ways that you can install packages. You can install them locally, as a folder off of your current project folder, or globally, so that the same package is available to all of your applications, regardless of where you located the project folder. There are many configuration options on how to override default locations and behavior, which we won't deep dive into now. In most cases, you'll install packages locally. There isn't much of a downside. If you are like me, you'll work on a project and get it working just fine and then want it to stay that way. If you install locally, you can have a pretty good feeling that your app won't get jacked up by you, or someone else, updating your packages to something incompatible. With a global install, you might end up shooting yourself in the foot by updating a global package you need for another project, thus breaking another project that is unrelated but uses that globally installed package. So, even though you might find yourself installing the same packages in several project folders, at least they can live independent of any other updates.

There *is* a way to save your bacon on your project dependencies: use a package.json file to list your project's dependencies, so that you get the correct packages and versions you need. There are a boatload of options available for a package.json, and we aren't going to explore them here. But this can give you an idea, at least, of what it would take:

```
{   "name": "IBM-i-socket-chat-example",   "version": "0.0.1",
"description": "Interactive chat app with IBM i",   "dependencies": {
"body-parser": "^1.11.0",   "express": "^4.10.2",
"socket.io": "^1.2.0"   } }
```

This is a package.json file from a project I have at GitHub (*https://github.com/phelgren/ rpg-node*). You can see how the project is defined. I gave it a name, version, and a clever description, and then I identified the versions of packages needed to run the code. The caret symbol (^) basically "locks down" the package version to the major/minor version stated. So in the example above, "body-parser" has to be at least version 1.11.0 but cannot go above a version 1.99.99. That is a way to keep from accommodating a version change that could have breaking changes. You can see the app also uses express and socket.io. So, package.json is a way to *try* to keep your projects stable in a very volatile, package-crazy world.

Yes, *now* we can take a look at some Node.js application building!

Just like any of the open source software we have looked at so far, Node.js can be installed on just about any platform. So if you are a Windows user, you can install there. If you are a Mac user, you can install there, and for you Linux folks, go ahead, make my day, and install it there. Node was originally part of the PowerRuby project (still is) but grew longer legs and is now a standalone product on IBM i. Python was originally needed as a scripting tool in order to install and compile other stuff, so we have a pretty robust, happy ecosystem in the IBM i world. I recommend that you install Node.js on whatever your "local" machine is because it is pretty convenient and is just drop-dead simple to deploy to IBM i whenever you need to "smoke test" an app in the IBM i world.

Installing Node.js is as "easy" as installing licensed program 5733OPS Option 1 on your IBM i. Easy as in "seems easy," and, as I mentioned elsewhere, installing the IBM i OSS product is a little different than normal. The first install of the product is a bit of a head scratcher because even though you may want to install only Node.js, the most humane approach is to add all 15 options at the time you install 5733OPS—in the future, you will thank me, even if six of the 15 options are currently placeholders. It's a good time to put on the latest PTFs as well, and it may take a bit of time because the IBM i OSS ecosystem is pretty diverse, and the prerequisite and co-requisite PTFs may hit quite a few other products.

Vexing Versions

The only thing you might run into as you move from one node environment to another is that the IBM i world isn't *quite* as progressive as the run of the mill Node.js world, so the version on IBM i might be slightly older than what you would find "in the wild." That is OK. Unless you are really pushing something to the bleeding edge, some version mismatching won't kill you. Node changed the version system it was using in late 2015.

There was a "fork" of Node.js into a new project called io.js in January 2015, and the two, though similar, headed in slightly different directions. The pre-fork Node.js was hovering around version 0.11.15, which my head says, "Wow! Long way to go to V 1.0!" My IBM i is running 0.12.13, and the current Node.js release is version 4.5.0. Confused yet? The IBM i version was a Node version released in ... March 2016, so it ain't all that old. What gives? Well, the fork of Node.js and Node.js itself "kissed and made up," and they combined the fork (io.js) back into the Node.js version. So, Node.js, a combination of the "old" Node.js and io.js, version 4.5.0, was released in August 2016. My guess is my IBM i version will soon be at 4.5.0 or greater (as I download PTFs in the background).

My Windows version of Node is 4.4.7, which is plenty compatible with what I am running on IBM i, so I build on Windows, deploy on i. I use the Sublime Text text editor as well, and IT uses Node to run JavaScript from the command line, so all is well and nicely unified. No worries!

Code! Let's take a look:

```
var httpsvr = require("http");
    httpsvr.createServer(function(request, response) {
      response.writeHead(200, {"Content-Type": "text/plain"});
      response.write("Hello World");
      response.end();
    }).listen(8888);
```

Our excellent JavaScript walk-through comes in handy here. First step in our Node script is to "require" http. The http module is included in the Node install; all you need to do is require the module, which is sort of like an OO version of a /copy in RPG. Require loads the module into the httpsvr variable, which is an object. In fact, we immediately make use of the methods present in the httpsvr object by invoking the createServer method! One line and voilà: we have an HTTP server!

createServer is passed an anonymous function, which has two parameters (objects), request and response. Then within that function, we invoke the writeHead on the response object, passing the value of 200 and yet another object, a name-value pair,

{"Content-Type": "text/plain"}. Without doing a deep dive on the HTTP protocol, an http response header must contain a status and a content type in order to be valid, so that is what we are going to give it, at minimum, at this point.

Wait a second: why are we dealing with a "response" when we haven't even *sent* anything to the server? Well, in this minimalist, scaled-down example, we are just going to have our server belch out some text as it starts up and receives *anything* on the listening port. What will we send? Ah, the requisite "Hello World" just to prove that it works. We follow that with a response.end method that basically flushes out the text. Notice the .listen(8888); at the end? That is an example of method "chaining" where multiple methods can be invoked on an object. In the case of the httpsvr object that we instantiated, it has many methods that could be invoked; we just took advantage of the chaining option.

We could have also done this, with the same results:

```
var httpsvr = require("http");
    httpsvr.createServer(function(request, response) {
        response.writeHead(200, {"Content-Type": "text/plain"});
        response.write("Hello World");
        response.end();
    });

httpsvr.listen(8888);
```

Some folks like the compactness of method chaining, and some like to indicate the invocation of each method explicitly.

If you were to save the script into a file called server.js, you could invoke it by typing node server.js at the command line (presuming the node binary is in your path), and ... nothing happens at the command line! That is because now the server you created is waiting for anything to hit that port. So head to your browser and type in localhost:8888, and magically, "Hello world" will appear. Drop ... dead ... simple.

The challenge, of course, is to move on to something a wee bit more involved. In my case, I already have something: the "chat" app I created a couple of years ago. Actually the "chat" app is to Node.js as the "blog" app is to Ruby/Rails. It is kind of the de facto standard of demo apps. So let's take a look at chat because it really does point out some of the features and concepts you would encounter in a more real-world setting. We'll start with the simple "Hello World," but you'll notice that it is slightly different from the "plain" node app:

```
var app = require('express')();
var http = require('http').Server(app);

app.get('/', function(req, res){
  res.send('<h1>Hello IBM i Node world!</h1>');
});

http.listen(3888, function(){
  console.log('listening on *:3888');
});
```

The obvious difference is the use of 'express'. Unlike http, express is *not* included with the base Node.js modules, so you'll need to use npm to install it. Again, I recommend that you do it locally to your project for now: npm install express@4.10.2. (I chose this version because I knew it worked.)

What express brings to the party is a bit more of a "framework" feel to the app. express *is* a Web framework, so we can use the methods it exposes to build our app. Could we have used a different framework? Sure! But express will meet our needs for this example. Let's get grounded in the example:

```
var app = require('express')();
var http = require('http').Server(app);
```

We are requiring express, and see that little () at the end? That is the weird self-invoking function, which in this case initializes the app variable. That second line is very familiar because we saw it in our "Hello World" Node.js demo script. In *that* case, we passed an anonymous function to the http module. In *this* case, we pass it the function handler Server(app), which will process the request and response parameters needed by the HTTP protocol. So far, so good. The next line is completely new:

```
app.get('/', function(req, res){
  res.send('<h1>Hello IBM i Node world!</h1>');
});
```

This is actually a "route," which basically says anything that is requested ('/') will get the following response sent back to the browser: "Hello IBM i Node world!" Later on, you will see the effects of routes more directly, but the route is part of a RESTful application. Finally, the last line:

```
http.listen(3888, function(){
  console.log('listening on *:3888');
});
```

just starts the app listening on port 3888 and also outputs 'listening on *:3888' to the console, so you know there is life there! So far, nothing radically different from our original "Hello world." Let's move on. We'll need a little more infrastructure for this step. Since we are creating a Web application, we'll need some HTML to frame and tart up the look and feel. Here is what we will use:

```
<!doctype html>
<html>
  <head>
    <title>IBM i chat demo</title>
  </head>
  <body>
    <ul id="messages"></ul>
    <form action="">
                                                    Continued
```

```
        <input id="m" autocomplete="off" /><button>Send</button>
    </form>
    </body>
</html>
```

Most of you folks are not Web monkeys, so the bits here may not mean much to you. But the short story is that we have an unordered list with an ID of "messages", which is just a placeholder for the list we'll be creating later. We have a form field with no action, and we have a single field for entering some value and a button.

I left out the CSS, but it will be used to decorate the HTML. I'll put it in a separate file and reference it in the HTML. We make the following change from a res.send method, which outputs an HTML string, and instead replace it with sendFile and point to our index.html file, like this:

```
app.get('/', function(req, res){
    res.sendFile(__dirname + '/index.html');
});
```

You can verify that it works by running localhost:3888 in your browser (or use the IP address of your IBM i; 10.0.10.205:3888 is the internal address for my i). So we have basically created a very fancy "Hello World" app so far. It really doesn't do much, but it looks pretty good. A chat app typically connects and communicates over a socket because there can be multiple folks chatting at a time, so we'll need some socket infrastructure in order to get the chat app built. Fortunately, there is a module for that: socket.io. npm install is our friend again here. Run this command:

```
npm install --save socket.io
```

Then we need to make a few modifications to our code. We'll add a bit of code that basically will be a "smoke test" on our socket connection and will emit "a user connected" to the console whenever we have a new connection, just like we see "listening on *:3888" after the server starts. Like so:

```
io.on('connection', function(socket){
  console.log('a user connected');
});
```

We also need to tart up our HTML and add a JavaScript reference to implement the client side of the socket. Our io object on the server implements the server side. Include this before the closing </head> tag:

```
<script src="/socket.io/socket.io.js"></script>
  <script>
    var socket = io();
  </script>
```

Now the server console will indicate when a user connects. We probably also want to have some indication when a user disconnects, so let's monitor for that and output to the console when that event occurs.

```
io.on('connection', function(socket){
  console.log('a user connected');
        socket.on('disconnect', function(){
          console.log('user disconnected');
  });
});
```

Still nothing real special here. All we see is connect and disconnect events. Nothing the least bit chatty going on at all. So let's add another incremental step. Let's take what is submitted in our message input element and output that into the console (baby steps!). I have added a little more infrastructure as well. I added the jQuery JavaScript library to add some more terse methods to keep the code compact. So we now have a bit more JavaScript in the HTML and a bit more JavaScript code on the server:

Server—io.on('connection'....):

```
io.on('connection', function(socket){
    console.log('a user connected');

    socket.on('chat message', function(msg){
    console.log('message: ' + msg);
  });

  socket.on('disconnect', function(){
    console.log('user disconnected');
  });

});
```

HTML <script>:

```
        var socket = io();
    $('form').submit(function(){
        socket.emit('chat message', $('#m').val());
        $('#m').val('');
        return false;
    });

    $( "#send" ).click(function() {
        $( "#txtmsg" ).submit();
    });
```

Note: The $("#...") references are the same as using the document.getElementById("...") methods in the DOM.

So what we have is a chat demo that only chats out to the console. Let's fix that!

The io.emit method is what we call when we want to send data out. If we don't qualify who the "emit" is for, it goes to everyone. All it takes is one more line of code on the server:

```
io.emit('chat message', msg);
```

HTML <script>:

```
socket.on('chat message', function(msg){
  $('#messages').append($('<li>').text(msg));
});
```

Compare that to the similar socket.emit method. In the example we are using, we "target" the 'chat message' client and send the data contained in the message input element. In the io.emit method (on the server), we send the data to everyone who is connected, and on the 'socket.on' method (on the client), we capture what was sent and use jQuery's append method to add it to the 'messages' (unordered) list element.

We have been walking through this piecemeal, so let's take a look at the whole tamale. First the HTML:

```
<!doctype html>
<html>
  <head>
    <title>IBM i chat demo step 6</title>
    <link rel="stylesheet" type="text/css" href="chat.css">

    <script src="/socket.io/socket.io.js"></script>
    <script src="jquery-3.1.0.js"></script>
  </head>
  <body>
    <ul id="messages"></ul>
    <form id=txtmsg action="">
      <input id="m" autocomplete="off" /><button id=send>Send</button>
    </form>
  </body>
```

Continued

```
    <script>
        var socket = io();
      $('form').submit(function(){
          socket.emit('chat message', $('#m').val());
          $('#m').val('');// clears the input element
          return false;
      });

      socket.on('chat message', function(msg){
        $('#messages').append($('<li>').text(msg));
      });

      $( "#send" ).click(function() {
          $( "#txtmsg" ).submit();
      });
    </script>
</html>
```

And then the 'server' JavaScript:

```
var express = require('express');
var app = express();
var http = require('http').Server(app);
var io = require('socket.io')(http);

app.use(express.static('public'));

app.get('/', function(req, res){
  res.sendFile(__dirname + '/index_6.html');
});

io.on('connection', function(socket){
    console.log('a user connected');
```

Continued

```
    socket.on('chat message', function(msg){
        io.emit('chat message', msg);
        console.log('message: ' + msg);// still outputting to console
    });

    socket.on('disconnect', function(){
        console.log('user disconnected');
    });

});
```

And a wee bit more stuff that makes the HTML look a little better in the chat.css file:

```
    * { margin: 0; padding: 0; box-sizing: border-box; }
    body { font: 13px Helvetica, Arial; }
    form { background: #000; padding: 3px; position: fixed; bottom: 0;
width: 100%; }
    form input { border: 0; padding: 10px; width: 90%; margin-right:
.5%; }
    form button { width: 9%; background: rgb(130, 224, 255); border:
none; padding: 10px; }
    #messages { list-style-type: none; margin: 0; padding: 0; }
    #messages li { padding: 5px 10px; }
    #messages li:nth-child(odd) { background: #eee; }
```

I also did something tricky along the way that we haven't talked about but *is* reflected in the code above. In the original version of this example, the CSS was included in the HTML. That is not an accepted practice except in the case that just a very few tweaks are needed. In this case, the CSS used is not extensive, but very often your CSS, JavaScript, and HTML reside in separate files so they can be individually maintained. So I put the CSS in a separate file, just as you would expect in a larger project. But that takes a bit of trickiness, as I said. You need to add the line:

```
app.use(express.static('public'));
```

So you can serve up your "static" files. Basically the code is saying that all of the static stuff will be found in the public folder, relative to the project folder you are running in. So the chat.css is living in there along with the jquery-3.1.0.js file. The <script src="/socket.io/socket.io.js"></script> reference is something different, though. The socket.io.js file lives in the node_modules/socket.io/node_modules/socket.io-client folder, but the initialization of the module "exposes" the file as though it were off the root of socket.io. Thus, it doesn't live in the 'public' folder like other non-module js files do.

System Access

So this is all very awesome IMHO, and actually any programmer would love this stuff. Easy, fast, flexible. But we IBM i folks have a bunch of stuff already written and living in the "alternate universe" of IBM i (OS/400)—so, how do we get to that stuff? If you read the chapter on XMLSERVICE, you should have an inkling of where we are going. There's a toolkit for that! But first, let's access the environment that Node.js lives in, and that is PASE. Getting to PASE is easy because it is the ocean we are swimming in. It is this easy:

```
const execSync = require('child_process').execSync;
var code = execSync('ls -l');

console.log(code.toString());
```

Much of what Node.js does is asynchronous, so in this case we are running a synchronous process—we will wait, thank you very much, for the output rather than including a callback to return the output when it completes. So that is what require('child_process').execSync is going to do: run a synchronous child process and return the output. That output comes in the form of a buffer of raw data, so we use the toString() method to get a string from the contents. Voilà! Our ls -l command returns the list of the files in the directory it is executed in. Easy.

Access to the IBM layer is a little more involved, but not much, because we already have libraries that wrap the XMLSERVICE routines, *and* if we need direct access to IBM i databases, we have libraries that can do that as well. The database access is a fairly straightforward process, one that may be familiar to you, so we'll start there.

DB2 Database Access

As I mentioned before, you don't have to slog through much here because the pioneers of Node.js and DB2 have gone before you. There is a library on your system (after installing 5733OPS) that is just waiting for you to use it. So let's do it!

```
var db = require('/QOpenSys/QIBM/ProdData/Node/os400/db2i/lib/db2');
var conf = require('./config.json');

try{

    db.debug(true);  // Enable Debug Mode if needed.

    db.init(function(){  // Initialize the environment for database
                         // connections.

        db.serverMode(true); // Enable Server Mode if needed

    });

    db.conn("*LOCAL", conf.username, conf.password, function(){
                            // Connect to a database

        db.autoCommit(true); // Enable the Auto Commit feature
                             // if needed.

    });

    db.exec("SELECT * FROM EMPLOYEE.EMPLOYEE ORDER BY EMPLNAME,EMPFNAME
FOR FETCH ONLY", // Query

        function(jsonObj) {  // Print the output in a readable way.

            // If you want to see the RAW JSON, get it this way
            //console.log("Result: %s", JSON.stringify(jsonObj));

            // Walk the array and object properties
            fLen = jsonObj.length;
                                                        Continued
```

```
            var createFirstRow = true;
            var header = ""
            var rowdata = "";
            var comma = "";
                   for (i = 0; i < fLen; i++) {

                       var jhash = jsonObj[i];
                       Object.keys(jhash).forEach(function (key) {
                             if(createFirstRow) // accumulate keys
                                 header = header + comma + key;

                       var value = jhash[key]; // accumulate row data
                       rowdata = rowdata + comma + value;
                       comma = ",";

                       });

                       // once a row is done output
                       if(createFirstRow)
                             console.log(header); // first line only
                       console.log(rowdata);
                       // clean out the row
                       rowdata = '';
                       // Turn off the header build routine
                       createFirstRow = false;
                       // clear out the comma
                       comma = '';
                   }
            }
      );

   } catch(e) {  // Exception handler

   console.log(e);

}
```

I tried to write this in a way that was generic and would output whatever table you decided to use in your SELECT statement. An additional idea that you could also implement here would be to output to a .csv file. But since we are, in most cases, going to be writing a Web app or something along those lines, the fact that the content is automagically formatted in JSON means that you'll get back an object from your database call, which is actually perfect for the Web environment.

A quick walk through the code shows you how simple it all is. Our first require line pulls in everything we need for database access into an object called db. So that is a pretty sweet start. The next require line I threw together because you probably don't want to hard-code credentials in your app. So I created a config.json file in the application's folder where you can stuff the username and password for connections. But don't stop there. The config.json file (it can be any name) can contain whatever you want: system name, database name, SQL settings, and so on.

The require('./config.json'); returns an object with the properties you defined in the file. (Hey! You are in objectland now, so a .json file is coming back as an object.) You reference the properties you defined using variable.property syntax. In my case, it is conf .password and conf.username. That file looks like this:

```
{
    "username" : "me",
    "password" : "secret_password"
}
```

All standard JSON stuff! Next we start a try block, so that if we have any errors we can catch and display them. Within the try, we set a couple of properties and initialize the db object. Next we use the conn method, passing in connection parameters. Then we run the exec method, passing in the SELECT statement. We could have just as easily issued a CREATE TABLE, INSERT INTO, DROP TABLE, or any other SQL executable statement within that exec method. In that same method, we also are passing in an anonymous function that will handle the results. It is actually within that function that we do the work of formatting the output.

The output comes back as an object, which is an array of objects. Each *row* returned is an object, and since those are all collected into a result set, an array is used to hold the objects. You can see the returned JSON by uncommenting the line that contains this:

```
console.log("Result: %s", JSON.stringify(jsonObj));
```

JSON.stringify renders the JSON object back into a string. I recommend that you also copy the output of that string, paste it into the text box found at *jsonlint.com*, and check it. It will "prettify" the output and validate that it is properly constructed JSON. Since we have an array of objects, our job is to iterate! So we grab each element in the array, using the key values the first time through to build a row "header," and then we get the properties of each object and concatenate all the values into a comma-separated row. Then we output the whole thing. All of it, except for the database I/O, is pretty standard JavaScript fare.

So, database access looks pretty simple. How about calling a program? Once again, I am thankful that the heavy lifting here was done by folks with spinning propellers on beanie hats that know a lot more about this stuff than I do. Most of that heavy lifting is encapsulated in a module, and it is using the XMLSERVICE library on IBM i to send and return the data needed for each call. Here is what I mean:

```
var xt = require("/QOpenSys/QIBM/ProdData/Node/os400/xstoolkit/lib/
itoolkit");
var conf = require('./config.json');
var conn = new xt.iConn("*LOCAL", conf.username, conf.password);

conn.add(xt.iCmd("RTVJOBA USRLIBL(?) SYSLIBL(?)"));

function cbJson(str) {

    console.log("The raw XML output --- ");

    console.log(str);  // Print the raw XML output

    console.log("The formatted JSON output --- ");
```

Continued

```
    console.log(JSON.stringify(xt.xmlToJson(str), null, 4));
                        // Print the formatted JSON output


}

conn.run(cbJson);
```

What I like about this example, which is found on the IBM developerWorks website, is that the output is displayed in XML as well as JSON format. But, look how little it took to get the command run and returned! Four lines of code, not including comments and formatting. Not much effort. The JSON magic is provided, right now, by the xmlToJson method in the iToolkit. That little ditty is needed because XMLSERVICE uses—well, XML! —to communicate. There is a "pure" JSON version of XMLSERVICE, which I hope goes through a name change before delivery (an XMLSERVICE library that used JSON would be ... weird). But perhaps, someday soon, you'll just be able to specify the language in your call, and it will "speak" whatever you tell it to, XML or JSON. The command call is very similar to other XMLSERVICE examples we have seen in Ruby, Python, and PHP. The RPG program calls should be just as familiar:

```
var xt = require("/QOpenSys/QIBM/ProdData/Node/os400/xstoolkit/lib/
itoolkit");

var conn = new xt.iConn("*LOCAL");

var pgm = new xt.iPgm("NODEDEMO1", {"lib":"OSSDEMOS"});

pgm.addParam("","1A");

pgm.addParam(0, "7p4");

console.log(pgm.toXML());

function cb (str) {

        // Print the raw XML output
                console.log(str);
```
Continued

```
            console.log("  ");
    // Convert the XML to an object
            var jsonback = xt.xmlToJson(str);
    // Print the raw JSON
            console.log("JSON: %s", JSON.stringify(jsonback));
            console.log("  ");

    var jsonback = xt.xmlToJson(str);
            jsonback.forEach(function(results,index){
                        results.data.forEach(function(data,idx){
                            console.log("Object type:" + data.
type + " value:" + data.value);
                    });
            });

}

conn.add(pgm);

conn.run(cb);
```

I am going to post the output as well because it will help you to understand the structure of the objects above. Remember, we are "bound" by the way the XMLSERVICE creates the XML output, and all we do is convert the XML to JSON to make for a happy transition to the JavaScript world where objects are king! Here is the output:

```
<pgm name='NODEDEMO1' lib='OSSDEMOS' error='fast'><parm><data
type='1A'></data></parm><parm><data type='7p4'>0</data></parm></pgm>
<?xml version='1.0'?><myscript><pgm name='NODEDEMO1' lib='OSSDEMOS'
error='fast'>
<parm>
<data type='1A'>C</data>
</parm>
<parm>
<data type='7p4'>321.1234</data>
```

```
</parm>
<success><![CDATA[+++ success OSSDEMOS NODEDEMO1 ]]></success>
</pgm>
</myscript>
JSON: [{"type":"pgm","success":true,"pgm":"NODEDEMO1","lib":
"OSSDEMOS","data":[{"type":"1A","value":"C"},{"type":"7p4",
"value":"321.1234"}]}]
Object type:1A value:C
Object type:7p4 value:321.1234
```

The call to the RPG program using XMLSERVICE is pretty standard. The first three lines load the module, connect to IBM i, and then create a reference to the program to be run on IBM i. The next two lines seem kind of weird because you'd think the program would know what the variables are. But, if you have grappled with the XMLSERVICE library and constructs, you know that it is pretty opinionated. In fact, it has to be opinionated to transition between the unstructured (in some cases) world of open source languages and highly structured world of RPG.

So we have to define the type of parameters passed as well as the values. In Java we would probably use Reflection to find out what the program object needed, but this is RPG, not Java, so we don't have an RPG program object that can tell us about itself. We define it. And, this is probably the most tedious and error-prone part of using XMLSERVICE. Fortunately, in this example we don't have many complexities, but some program or API calls can get pretty intense.

I created a callback function to be run when the data returns from the IBM i. This function handles the data coming back, the conversion of that XML into JSON, and then iterating through the objects created except for the conversion to JSON. But, the mystery may be in the code that iterates through the objects. Here is what the JSON looks like:

```
{
        "type": "pgm",
        "success": true,
        "pgm": "NODEDEMO1",
```
Continued

```
    "lib": "OSSDEMOS",
    "data": [{
            "type": "1A",
            "value": "C"
    }, {
            "type": "7p4",
            "value": "321.1234"
    }]
}
```

We have an object {} that has five properties: type, success, pgm, lib, and data. The data property is an array [], and that array has two objects. Those two objects have two properties: a type and a value. So if you were going to "draw" the structure of the object, it would look something like this:

```
returnedObj
            ==> data
                ==>object
                        ==> type
                        ==> value
```

or in "dotted" notation: retObj.data.object.type.

The kicker here is the data property. Remember that it is property of the object and an object itself. That is why when we iterate through the object array, the array is named data, and we have to use that name to get to the array. Hence the line that says: results .data.forEach(function(data,idx){ .... The reference to data seems to appear out of nowhere. In fact, results, which we named, has a property called data that we *cannot* change because it is a property of the object. data.type is the same way because both type and value are properties of the data object. Yeah, it can get a little hard to unpack sometimes, but jsonlint.com is your friend. When you paste your JSON into that validation window and hit *validate*, it will check your data and format it nicely. My original output becomes very readable after jsonlint.com gets through with it.

So, that should get you started in Node.js. We saw "bare bones" Node and a Node app that leveraged socket.io and express.js. We looked at calling PASE commands. We looked at database I/O, running IBM i commands, and calling IBM i programs. There is *so* much more I could walk through with you, but it's time for you to use *your* skills and imagination. There are tons of examples out there. Go explore and make them yours!

11

Apache and Tomcat on IBM i

This short chapter is here to get you grounded in using the Apache HTTP server in its particular implementation on IBM i and give you a bit of background and wisdom on that implementation. We'll also look at Tomcat, which is an application server that is written in Java and runs very nicely, thank you, on IBM i. I also thought about writing a chapter on Java for IBM developers. I decided against doing that, though, because there is a solid book, *Java for RPG Programmers* (MC Press, 2006), which covers much of what I would say. That won't stop me from talking about Java or even throwing you a Java example or two, but we won't go quite as deep into Java as I have into other open source languages because Java has been on IBM i for, well, it seems like forever. Java also happens to easily span the IBM i, PASE, and other worlds because you can run Java natively on IBM i or in PASE. My first foray into Java was, in fact, written using SEU (I think) and compiled using CRTJVAPGM. Oh, how far we have come!

So, just to draw the distinction more clearly for you: Apache, as an HTTP server, can serve up static resources such as HTML pages and can invoke programs to create HTML using Common Gateway Interface (CGI) standard programs like PHP and CGIDEV2. It serves up HTML and other Web resources very well, but it isn't serving up applications. In order to do that, you'll need an application server. I am partial to Tomcat because it has been around for quite a while, but there are other Java-based application servers out there. You get a tiny scaled-down version of WebSphere with your IBM i installation, and you certainly can install the full-blown WebSphere Application Server on your IBM i, but out of the box, you get Apache and not much more.

Apache is the latest incarnation of HTTP server on IBM i. Back in the early days when websites were run by hamster wheels and hand cranks, IBM's first foray into HTTP serving was a relatively clunky, native implementation based on the CERN HTTP server. I think this was available as far back as V3R2 and was called the "original" server when the HTTP Server (Powered by Apache) was introduced. The two servers maintained an arms-length relationship for a while, and eventually the CERN (original) implementation was retired. But, HTTP serving has been around on AS/400/iSeries/IBM i for a *long* time. Early on, most folks had no idea what to do with it.

Apache

What can you do with Apache? Well, since Apache is so efficient in serving up static resources and resources passed to it from CGI programs, you can leverage it for many things. I use it primarily as a reverse proxy for the plethora of programs, pages, and other plumbing in my Web apps (nice alliteration, eh?). What is a *reverse proxy*? A very handy little tool, in my humble opinion. If you are constrained on external IPs like I am (I get *two*!), then the ability to run multiple websites and yet pipe them to a single IP address is quite handy. My public-facing websites all share the same public IP, but behind the scenes, Apache directs them to their correct internal server instances—and I have a bunch of them running on my IBM i.

Here is an example of what my main Apache configuration file looks like:

```
# Configuration originally created by Create HTTP Server wizard on Mon
Oct 22 13:16:16 MDT 2012
LoadModule proxy_module /QSYS.LIB/QHTTPSVR.LIB/QZSRCORE.SRVPGM

LoadModule proxy_http_module /QSYS.LIB/QHTTPSVR.LIB/QZSRCORE.SRVPGM

LoadModule proxy_connect_module /QSYS.LIB/QHTTPSVR.LIB/QZSRCORE.SRVPGM

LoadModule proxy_ftp_module /QSYS.LIB/QHTTPSVR.LIB/QZSRCORE.SRVPGM

LoadModule proxy_balancer_module /QSYS.LIB/QHTTPSVR.LIB/QZSRCORE.SRVPGM
                                                        Continued
```

```
LoadModule zend_enabler_module /QSYS.LIB/QHTTPSVR.LIB/QZFAST.SRVPGM

Listen 10.0.10.210:80

AddType application/x-httpd-php .php .php5
AddHandler fastcgi-script .php .php5

AddType video/ogg .ogm
AddType video/ogg .ogv
AddType video/ogg .ogg
AddType video/webm .webm
AddType audio/webm .weba
AddType image/jpeg .jpg
AddType image/jpeg .jpeg
AddType image/png .png
AddType image/svg+xml .svg
AddType application/x-shockwave-flash .swf
AddType video/mp4 .mp4
AddType video/x-m4v .m4v

<VirtualHost *:80>
ServerName www.asaap.com
ServerAlias *.asaap.com
DocumentRoot /www/asaap

AddCharset UTF-8 .htm .html
DirectoryIndex index.php index.html

ProxyPreserveHost On
ProxyPass /asaap3 http://10.0.10.206:6080/asaap3
ProxyPassReverse /asaap3 http://10.0.10.206:6080/asaap3

ProxyPass /asaapwm http://10.0.10.206:6080/asaapwm
ProxyPassReverse /asaapwm http://10.0.10.206:6080/asaapwm
```

Continued

```
<Directory /www/asaap>
   Order Allow,Deny
   Allow From all
</Directory>

</VirtualHost>

<VirtualHost *:80>
ServerName www.valadd.com
DocumentRoot /www/valadd
DirectoryIndex default.html

<Directory /www/valadd>
   Order Allow,Deny
   Allow From all
</Directory>

</VirtualHost>

<VirtualHost *:80>
ServerName www.jrubyoni.com
ServerAlias *.jrubyoni.com
ServerAlias *.roroni.com

ProxyPass / http://10.0.10.205:3030/
ProxyPassReverse / http://10.0.10.205:3030/

</VirtualHost>
```

As you can see, or maybe you can't, I have several different server instances referenced here. Way at the top, the initial LoadModule directives are creating an environment where PHP apps could live, if needed. They load service programs from the ZendSvr library. I don't have any CGIDEV2 CGI pages that live in the main configuration, but I certainly do pass the traffic back to some CGIDEV2 sites. The next thing to pay attention to is the Listen directive, which is basically saying that this server instance is running on an internal address of 10.0.10.200 on port 80, standard for HTTP.

So, you might be thinking, if this is an *internal* address, how does the outside traffic get in? That takes a firewall, and I have one that is out there listening with an Internet-addressable IP on port 80. The firewall then maps that traffic back to my internal address (Network Address Translation—NAT—is the process). At that point, Apache is examining headers to see which Web address is being requested, so that it can figure which host to map the traffic to internally. I skipped over all the MIME types that Apache will allow in, but those are listed (mostly video and media files)—and the first virtual host is the *asaap.com* site. Note that *www.asaap.com* will be directed to the virtual host, but also *any* (*) host on the *asaap.com* domain will also end up here (for example, *mobile .asaap.com, demo.asaap.com*).

Finally, we see two reverse proxy paths that point to different subdomains. This happens to be a Tomcat server instance, so the two subdomains are actually pointing to two different applications running on Tomcat. So basically, if you typed in the URL of *www .asaap.com/asaap3*, it would be mapped to the asaap3 application running on Tomcat on port 6080 at the internal address on 10.0.10.206.

The beauty of the reverse proxy is that you can have all sorts of servers supplying resources to the same Web domain without anyone being the wiser. So I could also have a Web server running PHP but referenced in the *asaap.com* URL as *www.asaap.com/blog* and actually have it point to a WordPress instance running elsewhere on my network. Yet even though someone navigated from *www.asaap.com/asaap3* to *www.asaap.com/blog*, they never knew that they were changing servers. Very cool and flexible!

The other thing I have found helpful with using Apache for a reverse proxy is that by having a single "main" instance that receives all the traffic, it allows me to bounce a particular instance or change a configuration of that instance without losing *all* my websites. In addition, if all the servers serve sites that share the same domain, your configuration of SSL can reside on the "main" Apache instance with a wildcard certificate, encrypting all of your external traffic without the hassle of configuring SSL for every server instance you have. If you have PHP, Node.js, Tomcat, CGIDEV2, Rails, and some static resources as well, then a reverse proxy will just make life much simpler. And, in this business, simple is good!

What do CGI apps look like? Well, we can take a quick look at some CGIDEV2 configuration directives. You might see something like this:

```
# MobileREM directives
ScriptAliasMatch /mobilerem/(.*)  /qsys.lib/mobilerem.lib/$1
Alias /mobileremjs    /www/mobileapps/htdocs/mobilerem/js
Alias /mobileremcss   /www/mobileapps/htdocs/mobilerem/css


  <Directory /qsys.lib/mobilerem.lib>
    order allow,deny
    allow from all
    Options -ExecCGI
    CGIConvMode %%EBCDIC/EBCDIC%%
  </Directory>
```

In this case, the URL is mapping anything that follows the /mobilerem/ subdomain to the mobilerem library. So if I had a CGIDEV2 RPG program in the mobilerem library called mypgm.pgm, and the URL parsed looked like this: *www.mysite.com/mobilerem/mypgm.pgm*, then the directive above would execute the CGI program in the mobilerem library. Nice and flexible!

Tomcat

Apache Tomcat has been around for years. It was one of the very first open source programs I ever installed on my iSeries. I marveled that I could "install" something on that iSeries by just unzipping a file into the IFS. Fifteen years later, nothing has changed. I can get a Tomcat server instance going in less than five minutes. Here's how to do it.

Download Tomcat from the Apache Software Foundation website. Yes, Tomcat is an Apache product, which confuses the heck out of people because if you call it "Apache Tomcat" (which it is), they think you are talking about some derivative of the HTTP server. Nah! The Apache Software Foundation has a ton of projects, most of which go by the name "Apache (insert name here)." So, just go ahead and download the zip instance of Tomcat (or the tar..any archive) and unzip it into the IFS. I have an "Apache" folder in the root of the IFS, which currently has Tomcat 5.5.27, 6.0.33, 7.0.26, and 8.5.4 sitting in their own folders.

Once you've downloaded and unzipped Tomcat, you will need to make sure that the Java version you are running on your IBM i is compatible with the version of Tomcat you just downloaded. (Sorry, I guess you should have checked that first.) We'll make a brief detour now into Java-land:

There are *two* main versions of IBM's wonderful J9 JVM on IBM i: a 64-bit and a 32-bit version. Of course, you are thinking: 64 is better than 32, so let's go with 64! Not so fast, cowboy! In many cases, the 32-bit will outperform the 64-bit version. Unless you need to use a *lot* of memory for your apps, start with the 32-bit JVM. If it doesn't meet your expectations, switch to the 64-bit version. It is drop-dead simple to do so. And, *don't* rely on the IBM i environment to choose your JVM version for you. You never know when some nimrod will decide to change a systemwide value that points to a different JVM, and it will break your Tomcat instance.

Here is what I do: after unzipping the file into the IFS, I navigate down to the /bin folder and open the catalina.sh shell script. Then I add the following lines to the script (again this is Tomcat 8 running with version 8 of the JVM):

```
# Java 8 settings if needed export -s JAVA_HOME=/QOpenSys/QIBM/ProdData/
JavaVM/jdk80/32bit/jre export -s CATALINA_HOME=/Apache/Tomcat/apache-
tomcat-8.5.4 export -s JAVA_OPTS="-Dos400.awt.native=true -Djava.awt.
headless=true -Djava.version=1.8 -Xms256m -Xmx512m"
```

These directives are added at the very beginning of the shell script, just after the comments about all the options in the head of the script. They have never let me down. Then I launch this guy in a CL program like so:

```
SBMJOB CMD(QSH CMD('/Apache/Tomcat/apache-tomcat-8.5.4/bin/catalina.sh
   start'))   JOB(TOMCAT8)   JOBQ(QSYSNOMAX)
```

Couldn't be easier.

Tomcat is an application server, so the next step is to deploy your applications by dropping the .war files (Web Archive file) into the webapps folder. They automatically deploy. You are done.

So, that is the briefest of tours in the Apache HTTP and Apache Tomcat world on IBM i. I'll bet that most of your Web applications, whether they be PHP, Node.js, Rails, Python, RPG CGIDEV2, or even Java applications will probably sit in, or behind, the Apache HTTP server. At your service!

12

The IBM i Open Source Garden

If you have a garden, you might assume that there are gardeners about. When it comes to IBM i, we have plenty of resources to continue to till that fertile ground. Our community "gardeners" have established deep roots, so this chapter will just review what resources were available as of the time of this writing (2016). The "were" is because the open source world is not stationary. In fact, it seems, at times, frighteningly churning. Open source is not new, but open source on IBM i, as a supported product, is *quite* new, and the community has been playing catch-up. So I don't expect that any of this information will remain fixed. There are a few websites, mailing lists, and organizations dedicated to open source on IBM i, which have been around for decades and evolved nicely as the industry and our "midrange" platform continued to change. But, the past doesn't always predict the future, so take all of this information with a grain of salt. Missing websites and broken links are the bane and standard of the Internet.

I list these resources in no particular order. They are just what came to mind as I mulled over what is out there in IBM i OSS land.

User Groups

Alas! The whole concept of the "user group" has gone out of fashion, just like bell bottom pants. But although the Internet has displaced the "user group" as *the* place to get information and answers to questions, the "user group" is neither gone nor forgotten. Meet-ups have replaced the traditional user group, but some well-established groups continue to live on:

COMMON—This is a professional association that has been at the center of the midrange world, almost since it was established. Disclaimer: I was a COMMON board member for six years and continue to participate in and speak at COMMON events. This group is *my* idea of a solid leader among technical professional organizations. COMMON continues to hold live conference events as well as webinars, chats, roundtables, and virtual conferences, and the organization also offers professional certifications. The whole tamale!

OCEAN—The Orange County Educational Advancement Network, or OCEAN, is a great group in southern California. OCEAN holds many in-person events and has an active Web presence.

OMNI—Based in Chicago, these folks also have live events, a great Web presence, and a vibrant user community.

WMCPA—The Wisconsin Midrange Computer Professional Association, or WMCPA, includes two great user communities within 100 miles of each other. The heartland has heart!

LISUG—This is the Long Island System User's Group—see, we have coast to coast coverage! I haven't had the opportunity to speak to this group, but I know several of its members. It's another solid IBM i community.

Yes, there are many, many others. Do look for a group near you. The COMMON website tries to do its best in keeping its user group list up to date.

Virtual Communities

There are virtual communities (websites and lists) as well:

Midrange.com—This is the 800-pound gorilla of mailing lists for IBM i developers, admins, and hardware hackers ("Dr. Franken, I presume ..."). David Gates has nurtured this list along for many years (since it was a BBS). It has great posts and great moderators. This is really *the* place to stay in touch and be helped and informed. IBMers are known to lurk, too.

Club Seiden—Alan Seiden has a group that interacts at *club.alanseiden.com*. There are projects, chats, and lots to learn here.

LinkedIn—Of course! You know what LinkedIn is. Here is the link to the IBM i OSS group on LinkedIn: *www.linkedin.com/groups/8531863*.

Ryver IBMiOSS Group—More code, more chats, and more posts. This new group is found here: *ibmioss.ryver.com*. (This is a closed group, so you will need to create an account and then request permission to join the group.)

Litmis—Litmis (*www.krengeltech.com/litmis*) is a "side" business of Krengel Technology that Aaron Bartell, an active open source community member, is deeply involved with. Litmis is pushing the envelope of providing virtual IBM i OSS workspaces so that businesses can embrace OSS on IBM i. And he is sharing, too: code, code snippets, some documentation, tips, and some repositories for open source projects.

Notable "Solos"

There are some IBM i open source "rock stars" who have been contributing OSS to the midrange for a decade or more.

Scott Klement—Scott worked for his family business, which runs on IBM i, for years. While he was busy giving the business his best, he also shared his solutions with the community. Scott also wrote a prodigious number of articles and spoke at user groups and COMMON conferences. He currently works for Profound Logic (lucky outfit!). This guy is a machine! Check out his website: *www.scottklement.com*.

Aaron Bartell—When I grow up, I want to be just like Aaron! A younger mover and shaker in the community, Aaron seems to have been involved in just about every major endeavor in open source on IBM i for the past few years. Check out the whimsical Mow Your Lawn website, *mowyourlawn.com*, which has RPG OSS code and more.

Dr. Franken—is Larry Bolhuis. The good Doctor does unnatural things with iSeries/IBM i hardware (and who knows how far back). Well known for his IBM hardware exploits and the Frankeni website, *www.frankeni.com*, he has also teamed up with Pete Massiello and created the IBM i cloud hosting service: *iinthecloud.com/idev-cloud*. Nice!

There is a long list of other IBM i notables, speakers, writers, and hardware destroyers who are too numerous to mention. But, get *out* there and *get involved*, OK? I don't care how you do it. In person (the best IMHO) or online, it doesn't matter. But the IBM i community needs your input and participation. Not because it is dying, but because it is thriving and needs volunteers who can bring new ideas, new skills, and new ways of doing things. Boldly go where no developer has gone before, because you have the system to get it done. Use it!

Index

Boldface numbers indicate illustrations, code listings, and tables.